STORIES OF SURVIVAL IN BURMA WW2

by

Elizabeth Tebby Germaine

*Four beautifully written accounts of endurance and courage in 1942
when tens of thousands fled from the Japanese Invasion to India*

Published in 2016 by FeedARead.com Publishing

Copyright © Elizabeth Tebby Germaine

A CIP catalogue record for this title is available from the
British Library.

ACKNOWLEDGEMENTS

Grateful thanks to Paul, Priscilla, Margaret and Sue, the children of the late Stanley Farrant Russell, F.R.C.S. for permission to quote extensively from their father's out of print books, *'Muddy Exodus - A Story of the Evcuation of Burma, May 1942'* and *'Over the hills and far away'* Particular thanks to Paul for letting me have the use of much material looked after and recorded by himself from a collection belonging to 'Tommy' Thomson, Refugee Administrator of the ITA, Assam, 1942. Special thanks for permission to use the striking photos his father took during his dangerous journey. Thanks to the late Josephine Chapman who wrote a diary in 1941/42 and a book published in 1946 called *'Weathering the Storm.'* (Some material she wrote also appears in *'Distant and Dangerous Days in Burma and China'*.) Thanks to the late Dorothy Lewis for the unique collection of old photographs of Burma taken 1937-1966. Enquiries have been made to the publishers in India of the out of print book *'Out of the Burma night'* by Captain (Reggie) R H Gribble (1944).

This book has previously been published under the title 'DARK JUNGLE, STEEP MOUNTAINS'.

INTRODUCTION

This book combines four gripping and unforgettable stories written by people who lived through a dramatic and awful time in Burma in 1942. They escaped from the Japanese invasion of WW2 by walking through northern Burma – a remote area of dense jungle and high mountains – along with tens of thousand of other refugees of many races and the Allied forces who were forced to retreat. Thousands died on the way of exhaustion, illness and starvation.

At the time when Japan invaded the priorities in WW2 elsewhere in the world meant that military resources in Burma were inadequate. Also in the Far East it was necessary to defend the huge Allied naval fortress of Singapore which tragically was captured by the Japanese on February 15th, with the taking of tens of thousands of Allied prisoners of war. Much has been written about the unspeakable conditions in which these POW's lived and worked.

Despite the fact that the Imperial Empire of Japan had been invading and occupying parts of China for a number of years before WW2, in 1941 it was not generally expected that they would invade Burma. But air raids began on Rangoon shortly after the massive attack on the U S fleet at Pearl Harbor in December 1941 which brought the U S into WW2 and led to the declaration of war on Japan by Britain and the U S.

The first story, taken from a detailed diary, is what happened to Josephine Chapman, a British woman working in Burma. It gives vivid glimpses of Rangoon under attack, and the chaos that immediately gripped the country, with tens of thousands of people trying to leave by whatever means they could. Japanese troops entered Burma from the south and the east through Thailand and made very fast progress through the country. Her story takes us through Burma during the months of the first stage of the Burma Campaign, where she and her group were attempting the difficult and fraught journey. She arrived in Mandalay just before much of it was reduced to ashes by more savage air raids. Her own personal story was complicated by attempts to move some children to safety, and she ended up having to trek through the wild country areas with a group of strangers.

The second story was written by Captain R H Gribble of the Burma Frontier Force. During the first weeks of the invasion he was doing his usual December tour of the Hukawng Valley in the north which was soon to be overrun with desperate refugees and members of the military. In 1944 he published a remarkable account of his experiences in a book - *'Out of the Burma Night'* .

He had great knowledge and understanding of the Kachin and Naga people and their customs and ceremonies and wrote wonderful descriptions of the jungle. He was a forceful and decisive character who was held in great respect by the local villagers. In turn he valued their skills and way of life, describing individuals who helped him on his perilous journey. Many were later to fight with the Allies in the second stage of the Burma Campaign, which led to victory in June 1945, though that was not yet the end of the war in the Far East.

The third story was written by a surgeon who worked in a hospital in the small northern town of Mohnyin. Through a family connection with Burma I came to acquire a small out of print book *'Muddy Exodus - A Story of the Evcuation of Burma, May 1942'* by Dr Stanley Farrant Russell, F.R.C.S. This is a wonderful account of the experiences of his group in which were wounded soldiers who had been evacuated from a military hospital which had already been moved as the Japanese advanced. There came a point in April when all personnel were now told to get out of Burma by whatever means they could.

In the Foreword of *'Muddy Exodus'* Bishop A. T. Houghton wrote: *'....Dr Russell, whom we had known since boyhood after a brilliant medical course, came out in 1930 to organize and expand the promising medical work already initiated at Mohnyin. During the last twelve years his name had become famous over Upper Burma as a skilled surgeon, and many are the people of various races who owe their lives to the Mohnyin Hospital, and have there too learned for the first time the healing of the Great Physician, in whose name the work was undertaken.* (Although a surgeon and normally known as Mr Farrant Russell, in this book he is referred to as Dr Russell)

The fourth story was told in a long and detailed letter written by Sergeant Benjamin Katz, an RAMC orderly. Along with other soldiers he arrived at the tiny jungle village of Shingbwiyang in May 1942 and instead of struggling on with the journey he bravely stayed on and helped thousands of refugees passing through in appalling conditions. This letter is completely different from the other accounts, emotional, shocking, heartbreaking, funny and unforgettable.

Much of this book is based on material I was given by Dr Russell's son Paul. After reading his father's book I was able to trace him and he kindly handed me an astonishing collection of written records about this episode in history. This material had been in an old suitcase he was given, and had been put together by a much respected Administrator of Refugees from the Indian Tea-planters' Association, Mr R.M.Thomson, ('Tommy'). Paul had acquired these papers from Tommy's widow and had carefully sorted out and recorded much of it himself.

It was here I discovered Captain Gribble's book and the letter from Benjamin Katz.. Reports, letters, diaries, accounts, books and lists of names reveal a huge amount of detail about refugees and the several huge scale rescue missions organized by the ITA. Tommy Thompson ran the operation at Margherita in Assam co-ordinating dangerous and difficult expeditions to rescue refugees in trouble on the tracks over the high mountains of the Patkai range and through the Hukawng valley which deteriorated terribly during the monsoon. Many lives were saved in ghastly and terrible conditions.

The camp at Margherita was where Dr Russell, Captain Gribble and Benjamin Katz finally arrived after their exhausting journeys. Josephine followed a different route to the west ending up at another ITA camp near Imphal.

Paul lent me an exceptional book ' *Forgotten Frontier*' (1944) by Geoffrey Tyson. This contains much information about ITA operations and utterly incredible tales of endurance and heroism. Included are descriptions of a particularly dangerous and remote refugee route which went over the Chaukan Pass, further east than the ones described here and through areas of dense jungle where it appeared man had never been before.

Paul also let me have some striking photos taken by his father on his memorable journey many of which are included here. *'Forgotten Frontier'* also contains amazing photos (not included in this book). There are: views of the remote border country between Burma and Assam, the building of a new Manipur Road over the mountains into Burma, many brave porters on the refugee routes, jungle tracks, jungle camps, bamboo suspension bridges, meetings of ITA workers on the route, groups who attempted the very difficult Chaukan Pass route, elephants in swollen rivers, members of a party who came through this way including two POW's from Japanese camps who had escaped, perilous crossings over raging torrents balancing on slippery trunks of trees, Naga boatmen and boats which often had to be negotiated over fierce rapids, groups of the Assam Rifles, and a detailed map of the complex escape routes through jungles and over mountains.

'Forgotten Frontier' has Prefaces written by two Viceroy's of India who praised Tyson's account and the work of the ITA. Lord Lithlingow wrote one in 1942, and in 1945 General Wavell (then Viceroy) wrote – *'...No large scale migration of people can surely ever have taken place in worse conditions...the movement took place at the height of the monsoon in one of the wettest parts of the world; the country through which it was made could hardly have been more difficult. It was almost*

unknown, almost trackless; the thick jungle was infested with all the tropical plagues of mosquitoes, leeches, flies and similar pests; there were long steep ascents and descents; deep, swift, swollen rivers lay across the path; there were no local supplies of food available...'

There are as many stories – written and unwritten - as there were refugees. As with any records of events many years ago there are sometimes inconsistencies or facts that cannot be verified. Diaries and notes jotted down from day to day must have been used as a starting point. In the interest of maintaining the flow of the narrative I have left these as they are.

The whole journey was chaotic. Events were sometimes described from different viewpoints. Things might have been reported to have been said which were later contradicted, or plans were changed, and this may well have been when the speaker was suffering from extreme exhaustion, illness or hunger, or simple remembering it wrongly. Within groups travelling the road people sometimes appeared or disappeared without being introduced or explained. People varied who they walked with from day to day and contacts between Dr Russell's group and those travelling with Captain Gribble are sometimes unclear. Wilfred Crittle knew both groups and himself wrote an interesting account.

Opinions stated at the time were simply thoughts that individuals had in the extraordinary circumstances in which they found themselves, and we may disagree with them in hindsight or when looking at the bigger picture. For example, the Chinese troops released to help in Burma fought bravely alongside the Allies – but they were also the villains in Katz's story. They were hungry and far from home in the jungle and probably many did not know what was happening in the war during that frightening time.

Though there is one incident mentioned when they were handed paperwork. Katz wrote: *'... In our possession were maps and information written in Chinese for this Army's benefit. They were duly handed over. But instead of obeying the instructions and moving off to the spot where the Americans were dropping loads of rice for them, the devils just ate – and many died through overeating...'*

Many of the refugees were Indians, and Anglo-Indians who had made their lives in Burma over many years, finding occupations such as civil servants, traders and money lenders. There was an undercurrent of friction between them and the local Burmese population which added to their fear in 1942. Until only five years previously Burma had been administered as part of British India, only being made into a separate country in 1937. Civil unrest and armed uprisings were common, with nationalist movements and the rise of future Burmese leaders.

In October 1941 the Burmese Prime Minister, U Saw had travelled to London and met with Churchill to discuss the independence of Burma. This was deferred for the time being. (It was eventually achieved in 1948). On his return journey U Saw was arrested and detained by the British who suspected him of promising Burmese support for a possible Japanese invasion.

This book does not begin to pay tribute to all the many individuals who deserve recognition for their brave actions at this terrible time. In chapter 27 there are some descriptions of the remarkable rescue missions of the ITA and some of the huge dilemmas they faced.

Many brave lives were lost in Burma in 1942. It wasn't until later in the Burma Campaign that retraining and supply from the air changed attitudes to the fighting in dense tropical jungle and mountains. There was devastation and death on such a scale that the human mind cannot grasp it.

These accounts of refugee journeys carry us through. They are beautifully written by people who wanted to communicate their experiences. There are conversations, vivid descriptive passages, moments of humour and hope, often great sadness at having to leave Burma, and always the incredible human instinct to endure and survive. There were struggles and conflicts, uncertainties, illness, hunger, indecision, exhaustion and despair. Dr Russell never lost his belief that they were carried along by the hand of God. And there were unexplained incidents which happened like the four mysterious dogs who appeared from nowhere and guarded the food rations.

The photos are from a collection taken by Josephine's friend, Dorothy Lewis, (dml) and by Dr Stanley Farrant Russell (sfr) during his journey, with some provided in addition by Paul Russell (pr) from his family collection and some taken by myself (etg).

MAP OF UPPER BURMA

Some days after witnessing the bombing of Mandalay Josephine travelled further north and ended up trekking across to Imphal. The remote area through which the other three travelled to Ledo lies north west of Myitkyina, and modern satellite images of this part of Burma show vast areas of mountainous jungle where few tracks can be seen.

OLD PHOTOS TAKEN BY DR RUSSELL IN BURMA UP TO 1942

On the journey taking his wife and children to Myitkyina airfield to be flown to India he saw trains standing idle. He wrote: *'...On a siding beyond the station stood, disconsolately in a row, a dozen mighty engines. A brief time before in all their glory of green paint and gleaming brass, they had thundered north from Rangoon at the head of the Mandalay mail-trains ... the fastest metre-gauge engines in the world!...'* (Chapter 5)

Bullock carts

Many jeeps and lorries were abandoned on the first section of
track which was already waterlogged with early monsoon rains

A photo that survived when Dr Russell's camera fell into a river

'The final track to the refugee railway at N.Tirap, June 2nd 1942'

'... Some of my friends will never return, for they died on this the most extraordinary trek in history – a trek that caused untold suffering to thousands of people of many nationalities. Yes, how they suffered, young and old alike. It is astounding that so many survived and it shows in startling fashion the extent of human endurance when up against it...' Captain Gribble June 11th 1942 - from *'Out of the Burma Night'*

'...So many incidents Ted, that I cannot hope to include, although they are of interest. But the story I simply must tell! While the Chinese were here, four dogs appeared as if from nowhere. Each took up a position at the door of one bungalow. If any Chinese set foot in the compound, the dogs promptly went for him. Even General Tu was attacked, but we deemed it wise to stop the dogs before any damage was done to him. Where the dogs were fed, I don't know. They refused our food. Still they kept a vigil for 24 hours a day. Even now I cannot understand how this miracle came about...' From a letter written by Sergeant Benjamin Katz, a RAMC Orderly who stayed to help the refugees in the remote village of Shingbwiyang.

CONTENTS

Basha – wooden hut built of bamboo and jungle foliage
Duwa – respectful term for a Kachin elder or headman
Ga – village
Havildar – sergeant in the Indian Army
Hka – river
Jemadar – a Gurkha officer
Sepoy – private soldier In the Indian Army
Zup – confluence of two rivers or streams

CHAPTER ONE
December 1941

'"Mamagyi" said a voice, 'Here is a boy come across the fields...with a telegram' **Josephine**

Burmese landscape with boat and bullock carts (dml)

Josephine Chapman was an Englishwoman working in Burma in the 1930's. From a very large family, she had somehow got herself out of an office job, had studied for a diploma in theology and learnt the difficult Burmese language. She began writing a diary in December 1941 four days before Britain and the U S declared war on Japan.

On December 3rd she set out for the Irrawaddy Delta, catching the steamer from Rangoon and then rowing along small rivers and streams accompanied by a Karen boy. Her work took her to remote villages, but this time she felt uneasy about leaving Rangoon. Would she hear news? She tried to reassure herself by thinking that surely Japan would be exhausted after four years in China, and would not come this far.

In later days she mentioned collecting her daily newspaper, and she seemed well informed of events. Two days after it happened she heard that on December 7th the massive Japanese attack on the U S fleet at Pearl Harbor had changed the course of the war. She may not have known that attacks were also beginning on Malaya. These would lead to the Japanese capture of the great British fortress of Singapore, with the taking of thousands of Allied prisoners.

Unaware how world events were about to have a serious impact on her life and her very survival, Josephine was sitting in the schoolmaster's house in the village of Chaungwa and writing a Christmas play for the schoolchildren She described a peaceful scene, with the schoolmaster planting beans outside, and his wife bathing two small children in the river nearby.

'Mamagyi' said a voice, 'Here is a boy come across the fields from Nyaungngu with a telegram. He says too that the war has begun.' It seemed impossible that the war should disturb the peace of the villages. Promising to return soon, she rowed to Shwelaung, aiming to catch the night boat to Rangoon.

On December 12th she witnessed Rangoon's first air raid warning, while being nervously on ambulance duty. *'Nothing happened however.'* A few days later she was told to carry on with her work.

In Malaya many believed that the dense jungle would obstruct Japanese soldiers from progressing through the country. But the Japanese had close air support and were more experienced in warfare in the difficult terrain. They used bicycles and light tanks and advanced swiftly towards Singapore.

In the next few weeks Josephine was to travel to many places until it became too dangerous and she too was to get caught up in the general exodus of people travelling northwards. On December 21st she returned to the Delta village where she and the schoolmaster rehearsed their plays. Two days later they saw planes flying across and people were unsure whether they were British or Japanese. She heard news from the river steamer the next day that air raids had killed hundreds of people in the streets and docks of Rangoon.

There were Christmas gatherings of the village people, and she went off to Gayan meet friends on Christmas Day. *'...Rowing along the streams between the long grass and the bamboos, watching the multi-coloured birds and the fleecy white clouds in a blue sky, it was hard to think that the world was at war...'*

On Christmas Day many Christians gathered for a service, and later more Japanese planes flew overhead. Rangoon had its second air raid. She met friends and arrived back in Rangoon on December 27th. These brutal and unexpected attacks very quickly reduced the local population to chaos and indecision. *'...The docks and streets were deserted and there was no transport of any kind. Bazaars and shops were also shut and I discovered later that essential workers from hospitals and post offices had fled. S. Mary's Letter Street and S. John's College had been evacuated because of unexploded bombs in the neighbourhood...'*

She heard how friends had been on ambulance duty and had driven through exploding bombs and machine guns, and a student she knew had been killed. People were travelling in all directions. David Paterson was to become an army chaplain, while others were to travel north to Shwebo.

One of the Japanese aims in invading Burma was to take control of the Burma Road.   This was a supply route from Rangoon up the railway and across on a spectacular mountain road through to China. The U S and Britain were sending supplies to help the Chinese fight the Japanese invasion of the east of China and many ports.

In a book published in 1946, Josephine wrote: *'In a hollow of the Shan Hills 120 miles from the border of Yunnan lies Lashio, which for two thousand years has been a halting place for caravans of traders crossing the mountains on their way to and from China.....In modern days this caravan track has been widened into a motor road;   and when the Burma Railway was built northward from Rangoon, Lashio became the terminus. From there eastward into China the country was considered too mountainous and steep, too wild and disease-ridden for the building of a railway.   Lashio grew accordingly; and during the days before the war when the amount of traffic on the road increased, buildings sprang up on the hill-side almost as quickly as mushrooms grow in the night.*

The inhabitants of Lashio are people of many races. Some are rich merchants, some small traders. Some keep inns and shops and garages for the benefit of the travellers, and some work on the railway.....'

The building of the Burma road was a massive achievement, developing the old Chinese trading route over high mountains and through deep gorges. In a radio broadcast in Hawaii, 1940, King-chau Mui the Chinese Consul-General at Honolulu had compared it with the massive task of constructing the Great Wall of China. He paid tribute to the 200,000 local Burmese and Chinese workers who in 1937 had worked long hours with very little modern equipment, overseen by Chinese engineers who had studied at American universities.

The work involved building almost 300 bridges and nearly 2000 culverts. The road was open to traffic in 1938 after 8 months of work. Its twists and turns take 715 miles to cover its precipitous route, a distance of about 300 miles as the crow flies to reach Kunming in Yunnan, the ancient Chinese city built on a high plateau and surrounded by mountains.

DECEMBER 1941

While Japanese air raids were happening in the south of Burma, in the north reports of the war seemed remote. Captain R.H.Gribble was also going to be on the move a great deal in the next few weeks. In December his work in the Burma Frontier Service usually involved a tour of the jungle clad country, and this was to be complicated by demands on him to supervise arrangements to build another road.

My headquarters were at Kamaing, a little Shan-Burmese fishing village in the northernmost district of Burma, close to the mighty mountain ranges that extend higher and higher into the snowy regions bordering on Tibet.

The village boasts one motorable road connecting it with the Burmese railway town 25 miles to the east. The country is covered in dense tropical jungle and traversed by numerous rivers. This thick green wall of jungle also engulfs an area known as the Hukawng Valley, some 100 miles to the north-west. Beyong this again lies a formidable range of mountains known as the Naga Hills – a semi administered area inhabited by head-hunting tribes people called Nagas.

Every year, round about Christmas time, it was customary for an expedition to set out to the Hukawng Valley to meet the Shan and Kachin inhabitants and to aid them in the administration of that territory through the medium of the Kachin tribal chiefs.........I was glad of the opportunity to make another tour to the Hukawng Valley which in some strange fashion seemed to be beckoning me back to the shelter of its great forest, leaving the war and threats of war to those more directly concerned with the Japanese menace.

Few would have cared to prophesy that within a few months the Japanese monster would have stretched its mechanised head through the heart of the northernmost district in Burma and that thousands of refugees would have sought safety in the wilderness to the north-west.

In the meanwhile my little expedition got together: the mules arrived, the Travelling Dispensary was ready. The Kachin Police dressed in Khaki with blue puttees and red head-dress reported for duty. Supplies were purchased, for in the Hukawng it was quite impossible to obtain rations of any decription.

A few days after Christmas 1941, in glorious weather, we set out on our peaceful adventures. In the quietness of the jungle we almost forgot the war......On the third day the column reached Shaduzup, a picturesque Kachin village situated on the bank of a gurgling, glistening mountain stream. A delicious spot for bathing. Even the village maidens visiting the river to fill their bamboo water-pots, did not hesitate to fling off their clothes and glide naked into the running water, where they splashed and joked and laughed in the sunlight, until it was time to fill up the water-pots and wander back to their homes, refreshed and ready for a strenuous day's work.

...In the evening I met the village Elders and discussed local affairs with them. The crops were good they said, but wild elephants were a nuisance. Could they shoot a particular tusker who had even gone so far as to push his head through the wall of a house and search for paddy? Certainly, I said, it was up to them to protect their food supply...

..I entered one of their houses and sat by the white ashes of the fire in the 'hdaw dup' (guest-room) and was offered some 'shiru' (rice beer) served in a bamboo cup. Cheerful, happy and hospitable, I could not but envy them their fortunate freedom from the outside distorted world called civilization.

These simple jungle folk do not reason beyond the bounds of superstition. They are essentially Nat (spirit) worshippers and whenever death or sickness dogs a house some offerings are made to propitiate the spirits. Maybe a buffalo is slaughtered. Should this fail to have the desired effect, a priest (Dhumsa) is consulted. He performs a somewhat elaborate ceremony with short bamboo sticks which are heated in a fire until they burst. The fibrous hairs are then interpreted by the priest. By his aid the particular Nat who is the cause of the illness is discovered and propitiated, with eggs, fish, spirit, or the flesh of a pig. One definite result is that the villagers are continually deprived of valuable livestock; which leaves them extremely poor.

...After passing the low hill known as Jambu Bum and in an ever darkening forest, with the rustling of the tropical leaves and the indefinable stir of the oncoming night audible everywhere, we made camp in a forest clearing alongside a small water course. I had noticed during the course of the day that the track had become pitted with round holes sunk six inches into the ground, with large fresh rolls of brown dung scattered here and there. It became apparent that elephants were in force, feeding on the bamboo clumps that had now become prevalent.

Precautions were taken to light large fires in the camp and to burn bamboos at intervals. Bamboos being hollow inside let off when heated, loud reports, and this noise was usually successful in scaring away the denizens of the jungle, at any rate until such time as the sentry fell asleep!

DECEMBER 1941

A view of the jungle   (used on the cover of this book)   (dml)

Suddenly in the middle of the night, without any warning, the whole forest was echoing with the most awful noise I had ever heard. It was like the screeching of a dozen air raid sirens, deafening, bewildering. I hopped out of bed and seized my gun. In a few seconds the Kachin Durwan came running to my tent and gasped out that an elephant had broken down his hut and was searching inside for paddy (unhusked rice).

We raced together in the direction of the Durwan's hut. I shone a torch and there, right in front of me, framed in the green foliage, I saw a tusker. The animal's trunk was waving backwards and forwards, its great ears were spread out from its head like flapping fans. How huge that animal looked! I was only armed with a shot gun when he came charging towards me. I flung myself desperately through the tangled growths, while the elephant went crashing through the jungle. There was hubbub in the camp and several guns went off. There were a number of elephants in the herd which scattered into the jungle, the sound of the animals growing more and more distant......

'*...From the large Shan village of Mainghkwan which is the centre of the universe in the Hukawng, tracks radiate in all directions. But the one that we shall be more than interested in runs north to the Chindwin river (Tanai Hka) at Taihpa, and thence to Yupbang, a village on the banks of the Tarung Hka – river of death – 8 miles further on.*

In the dry season there are raft ferries at the crossing of both these rivers. The track then turns west and continues another 25 miles until it reaches the dreary little Kachin village of Shingbwiyang at the foot of the eastern range of the Naga hills. The reader should remember this little place is it presently assumes an important out of all proportion to its size.

...in order to encourage the younger generation to take interest in worldly affairs an elementary school was established in the Valley. This year, 1941-1942, I had the pleasant but difficult task of selecting a number of sons of Kachin chiefs for education outside the Valley.

On his travels Gribble discussed disputes and problems and gave advice '*...the Shans in some instances intermarried with the Kachins. This resulted in the spread of Buddhism throughout the Hukawng and the entry of a few Kachins into the monasteries in Burma for study and putting on the yellow robe. One Shan-Kachin monk even established his headquarters at a monastery in the valley and became a power in the land.*

In more recent years some European medical missionaries of the

BCMS settled in Mainghkwan. The Kachins therefore had three religions from which to choose. If they elected to become Christian, they had to do so one hundred per cent. The bulk of them, however, were attracted by Buddhist ritual and festivals, added to which it was not necessary for them to give up worshipping Nats or Spirits, of whom the number is endless, and the result has been that most of the animist villages in the valley boast of a Pagoda as well as Nat shrines.

Old photo on which is written *'Naga School'* (dml)

Gribble was riding his white pony, 'Topsy'. ...*Early one morning I set out for the tiny Kachin village of Shingbwiyang......Who would have thought that in the short space of three months this dreary little village was to become the centre of a seething mass of tortured humanity, ready to face starvation and the terrors of the jungle rather than fall into the hands of the Japanese invaders of Burma, whom they knew to be an incredibly cruel and barbarous foe, incapable of any decency of feeling, and whose idea of "sport" was to toss babies on the points of their bayonets, and to slaughter prisoners in cold blood, as if they were sacks filled with sawdust.*

When I arrived at this little village on a lovely cold sunny morning in January, coming events had not yet cast their shadows before. I went there to enquire into illicit trading in opium, and to make the acquaintance of some Naga chiefs for the first time... That evening as the sun began to dip behind the range of hills in the near distance, Ma Roi came over to my tawmaw (rest hut) and sat near the fire burning brightly at the foot of the steps.

Ma Roi is the name of a young Naga girl. Her parents lived in the hills, but she told me she was on a visit to some relations in the Valley, and hearing that I had arrived and was in possession of a radio she came across from the village in the hope of hearing some Burmese music. She was dressed in a short black skirt consisting of an oblong piece of cloth with a narrow fringe of embroidery, and a white sleeveless jacket, and her hair was gathered into a knot and brought up in front of her head like a horn with a silver button on the top. She was a talkative, provocative little person, and as she sat there before me the sound of her laughter was the prettiest thing imaginable in the stillness of the forest.

Ma Roi told me that her father was Chief of a tract in the Naga Hills, and suggested I ought to go and see her village, noted for its beauty, and added that when she was a baby a certain important officer whom she called 'Pawtah Duwa' sometimes carried her in his arms. I smiled at her and remarked that she was now too grown up to be carried. She thought this over a moment and then with a ripple of laughter she moved swiftly away in the direction of the village.

It was not the last time I saw her. I met her again a month or two later when the modern world was to convert this little jungle village into a place of horror....

...Of all the Chiefs who came to see me at Shingbwiyang, Sambaw soon caught the eye. He had an agreeable bearing and it was soon to be proved that he was a man of the most excellent sense and steadiness.

He was a Naga Chief, and a respectable one, for he did not belong to the branch of his race that indulged in headhunting. In his youth he had wandered into Burma, where he was attracted by the Yellow Robe and admitted into a monastery. He learned to read and write Burmese fluently and became a Friar of the Holy Order. After the death of his father he returned to the Hills and took over the administration of a large tract.

No longer did small parties set out in search of human heads. This enlightened Chief made it plain that his villagers must confine their activities to the collection of animal heads for religious observances...

....while I was in conversation with Sambaw, a terrific reverberating explosion was heard some distance to the north of the camp, the noise of the explosion echoing and re-echoing among the hills like the booming of artillery. "A Kachin gun," I said, without blinking, but Sambaw was not

so easily deceived. "The Dukaba has many times heard a Kachin gun fired," replied Sambaw, "and one hundred such guns would not make so much noise. I hear rumours of a war with Japan. Will the Dukaba tell me about it?" It was no use trying to bluff Sambaw, and I told him that the Japanese were at war with the British Empire and that the terrific noise we had just heard might have been a bursting bomb....I did not know it then, but before long I was to see a good deal more of Sambaw in the most extraordinary, unforgettable circumstances, when he and his villagers were to be my companions for several weeks and by their aid I was to escape from Burma over the Naga mountains into Assam.

A few days later after settling more disputes in the villages he wrote:
'That night I issued orders to resume the journey at dawn. The night air was cold and we sought the warmth of our blankets at an early hour. However it was not to be a restful night, for shortly after 1 a.m. I was awakened by the sound of voices unusually noisy at that hour. I got up, thinking there might be a quarrel, and lifted a flap of the tent, saw lights moving around. They gradually got clearer, brighter as some shadowy figures moved in the direction of my tent. Soon I recognized the clerk Duli as he approached, followed by several Kachins.

"An urgent letter for you, Sir" he said, handing me a buff coloured envelope. "These villagers have come by forced marches to deliver the letter without delay." I opened the cover and found inside an official telegram requesting me to return to Headquarters by forced marches. There was another cover, containing a letter requesting me to try and get into touch with two war correspondents, who apparently intended to travel on foot through the Hukawng and Naga country to India.

The war is getting closer, I thought to myself, but to Duli I merely said. "We have to get back to headquarters as soon as possible. Tomorrow we march all day."

By this time the Japanese were advancing through Burma on several fronts. The extreme loyalty to their Emperor and fanatic courage of their forces were to make them one of the most feared enemies in WW2. In a speech at this time Churchill referred to them as *'...a vast military empire..., with more than seventy mobile divisions, the third Navy in the world, a great Air Force, and ....eighty or ninety millions of hardy,warlike Asiatics'.*

In the South China Sea the battleship HMS Prince of Wales, the battlecruiser HMS Repulse were sunk by the Japanese making the east coast of Malaya vulnerable despite being defended by Indian army units. From Dec 29th there were more frequent air raids on Singapore resulting in thousands of civilian casualties.

Rev.Wilfred Crittle also lived and worked in Kamaing, and was known to Captain Gribble He wrote: *'...As far as we personally were concerned it was the loss of the 'Prince of Wales' and the 'Repulse' that first shook us. It was this that more than anything else opened our eyes to the fact that we were up against a really first class enemy. Prior to that the feeling may perhaps be best summarized in the words of a senior government officer whom we met on the train, "I should not think that they will give us much trouble. It will probably be over in six months!" It was not in the way that we had imagined. Even at that time however the more thoughtful people in Upper Burma deprecated the bombastic tone of many newspaper articles and radio broadcasters...*

CHAPTER TWO
January 1942

'…already I fancied I could see signs of a tremendous and imminent upheaval in these hitherto dark, overgrown jungle places which for thousands of years had remained undisturbed…' **Captain Gribble**

By January 1942 Josephine had witnessed the air raids in Rangoon and with so many people she knew on the move she felt rather alone. She went to stay at Bishopscourt. She saw schools being closed or moved to what were considered safer places, though what people didn't yet know was that nowhere would be safe for long.

Old photo of a boys' school during British rule   (dml)

'… a frantic rushing hither and thither became the main occupation of the rest of Burma. Townsfolk fled to the jungle; Rangoon went to the hills and then changed its mind and came back.. Folk from the hills came to Rangoon en route for India, but hearing of a boat sunk in the Bay, returned home again to await further developments. There was congestion on boats and trains going in every direction, and everybody was fussing around wondering whether Upper Burma or India were better. And meanwhile ugly clouds were gathering on the Siam horizon, thirty miles from Moulmein…'

Burmese Military Police guarded the border with Thailand but were thinly spread over a wide area. Many Japanese troops approached from Thailand, and from the start their air force dominated the skies. Josephine went to Prome for a tour of Chin villages but she and Saya Kya Bu had trouble finding transport. Prome was packed with refugees from Rangoon and there was an air raid warning while she was there.

She returned to Rangoon in the middle of January to take some schoolchildren to Pakokku. This would already have been a long way to go, but trains were now overloaded, and it took them 36 hours to do a 12 hour journey, '...*followed by a 6 hour journey in bullock carts across the sands of Myingyan on the dustiest road I have ever travelled and a five hour journey by river on a a very crowded boat...*' She met a District Superintendent of Police on the way who said he thought it was a waste of effort to open up the country schools, and she commented later that at the time she didn't take him seriously. When she returned to Rangoon – '...*the city was emptying fast and the Japanese were advancing, Moulmein, Martaban, Bilin River, the Sittang.*'

There were heavy Japanese air raids on the colonial town of Moulmein east of Rangoon, and many people fled to surrounding countryside. After much brave fighting there was an evacuation of most Allied personnel in fifteen paddle steamers of the Irrawaddy Flotilla Company and the Japanese took control of the town and the airfield.

There were night raids in Rangoon. Some Europeans waited for a boat to England, some were still in the Delta. Josephine went off again touring villages, including Yeleggi, travelling this time in a ' ramshackle old car.' The Karen Christians were afraid of the Burmese Buddhists and there was talk of many Burmese in the villages supporting the Japanese.

At the end of January and back in Rangoon she collected bread and the daily newspaper and went to a service in the Cathedral, then went five miles to collect a YWCA hostel key. The middle of town was quite deserted.

Old photo of Pagoda Road Rangoon   (dml)

Josephine was sorting out crockery when there was an air raid warning and she had to shelter in a police station. Later she met other colleagues in a trench, including George Tidey who later had to trek through the jungle in the Hukawng valley, and was in touch with Dr Russell and other groups. She felt overwhelmed with uncertainty about her own future.

Captain Gribble was travelling back from the jungle village to his headquarters after receiving the telegram telling him to return. There was news of a plan to build a motor road through the Hukawng Valley – like many such plans at this time of huge upheaval amongst the population, work was begun and then suspended. ...*We completed the journey to Mogaung on foot and caught the sugar-train about 8 a.m. the next morning....The sugar-train ...was in no hurry to complete the journey of 40 miles to the north, but I eventually reached my destination about 3 p.m., hungry, tired and impatient; but I could still boast I was the captain of my soul, but only just. Seven hours in which to cover 40 miles! "Good heavens," I thought, "My mules were capable of putting up almost as good a performance." At 4.30 p.m. I was summoned to an important conference....*

...At Myitkyina I heard the startling news that an enormous number of labourers would soon be arriving at my sleepy little headquarters (at Kamaing), with the object of building a motor road through the dense forest country of the Hukawng to connect with India. Pending the arrival of the multitude of labourers, two Chinese Engineers would make a preliminary inspection of the mule track. As I was familiar with this territory I would accompany them and, time being precious, we would make the journey to the Hukawng by bus, a distance of 104 miles. We were encouraged to make this adventurous journey by motor vehicle because a passenger bus had quite recently accomplished the journey along the mule track in 8 hours.........Early one morning we set out in two heavily loaded lorries, hoping to reach Mainghkwan the same day.
　All went well until we reached a village a few miles south of Shaduzup. At this place a bamboo bridge about 200 feet long spanned the Nanikawng river. It was a perfectly good bridge for mules but was never intended for motor traffic.
　There followed descriptions of one lorry collapsing into the river.
　'*...While the energetic and able Burmese drivers and their assistants were busy clearing away the debris I walked up to the village to seek the help of the Akyiwa and his villagers in order to cut a track down the river*

bank and up the other side to make it possible for my own lorry to cross. We were determined to go on; there was no going back. All worked cheerfully and with a will, Chinese, Indian, Kachin and Burmese. In three hours both the lorries were safely across and on the other bank.....From Shaduzup onwards the forest grew incredibly thick, and consequently the track was not sufficiently recovered from the rain to make the rest of our journey an easy one...

... We spent a whole day filling holes, and covering patches of mud and pools of water with branches and leaves cut from the jungle, alternately hauling one or other of the lorries out of the mud. It was only towards evening that we came in sight of the purple wooded mountains outlined faintly to the north of Mainghkwan. We reached camp as the red glow in the sky faded slowly into grey.

The next day I discussed with my companions the possibilities of making a new road, and also preparations for continuing the journey on foot to the formidable hills visible in the distance. They now informed me they had seen enough of the track to make it hardly necessary to go any further. The nearness of the rainy season and the boggy nature of the Hukawng Valley indicated that their hands would be full for quite a considerable time. They would utilize a day or two writing reports and drawing sketches after which they would be ready to return whence they came.

This arrangement suited me. In fact I felt relieved for already I fancied I could see signs of a tremendous and imminent upheaval in these hitherto dark, overgrown jungle places which for thousands of years had remained undisturbed. Was that dark and vast expanse of forest that had lain so long in a dull sleep to be disturbed at last? Without much stretch of imagination I could already hear the footsteps of countless human being as they tramped hurriedly, desperately through that dense dark forest country.....

'Don't tour anymore,' said Daw Pwa Sein, 'It might be dangerous for you… **Josephine**

Josephine was attempting to carry on as usual, but this was no longer possible. She was still in Rangoon, and there was the constant need to shelter from air raids. A church was damaged, *'… a few broken windows and some damaged woodwork and much dust…'* Some people she knew were now in the army - Po Khin and Ba Shein.

In early February despite the dangers around her she travelled again to the Delta to Nyaungngu to see women she knew, Daw Pwa Sein and Ma Thit and part of a school, St Mary's, Kemmendine that had been moved there. She saw Saya Po Taw who ran a Teaching Training course.

There were Japanese propaganda pamphlets being dropped, with '… *a caricature of two Burmans tied to a tree and an Englishman in the act of shooting them. Above was written; 'Let us destroy these English who kill our heroes.'* People asked her what they meant. She believed they referred to school strikes and riots that had happened two years previously. It is possible she had at some time witnessed the brutal treatment of Burmese demonstrating against the British.

Through these weeks Japanese attacks on Singapore intensified and Allied communications on the island were disrupted. Many Japanese landed during darkness, exploiting weak links in the forces defending the island. Churchill sent a cable to General Wavell saying that the battle must be fought to the bitter end with what he perceived as the greater numbers of the Allied forces.

After a few days she was on her way back to Rangoon again. The night steamer was still travelling to and fro, though later all the famous old steamers of the Irrawaddy Flotilla Company were destroyed to prevent them falling into enemy hands. The Karen lad who rowed the small boats with her was fearful to carry on – Karens and Burmese who associated with the British were to be in greater danger if found by the Japanese. He was going back to his own village and she felt sorry for him.

Daw Pwa Sein was a Burmese woman in her later 40's who had converted to Christianity against her father's wishes, and had become a much loved head teacher in the British school system. She was later to be killed by Burmese Buddhists who heard she and others had looked after British soldiers who had arrived confused, tired and hungry in their village.

She advised Josephine, *'Don't tour anymore… 'It might be dangerous for you, and dangerous too for the Christians with whom you were found. We shall be alright.'* Josephine knew of one British missionary who was still in the Delta caring for mothers and babies.

The struggle for Singapore was drawn out with huge civilian casualties and fears that the water supply would run out. Japanese troops entered the Alexandra Barracks Hospital where there were brutal massacres of patients and wounded troops.   Finally on Feb.15th there followed the largest surrender of British-led military personnel in history. Tens of thousands of British, Indian and Australian troops were killed or became prisoners of war of the Japanese alongside many taken earlier in the Malayan Campaign.

Back in Rangoon in the middle of February hospitals were being evacuated and services had ground to a halt.   The city was almost empty. The Evacuation Office was on the point of moving to Mandalay. Josephine mentioned various colleagues who were helping with these arrangements.

She heard that the Sittang Bridge was destroyed. The Battle at Sittang Bridge happened on Feb.19th - 23rd. This disaster for the Allies has been referred to as the most decisive battle in the first phase of the Burma Campaign, with significant losses for the Indians,   British   and Gurkhas.   She wrote: *Pegu would be next and the railway, and Rangoon would be cut off.*

A street in Pegu   (dml)

Josephine became preoccupied with thoughts about the safety of children from a Bishop's Home in Rangoon who had already been moved to Kyaukse, halfway to Toungoo in central Burma. Her involvement with efforts to look after these children was later to lead to complications on her own journey, and eventually caused her to miss a chance to fly out of Burma on one of the last evacuation planes from Myitkyina. Many of her colleagues escaped to India on these planes .

On February 17th she agreed with a colleague to go and try to help with arrangements, but then she heard that the Evacuation office were collecting children and schools as they travelled through Burma on a train. She began to talk in terms of getting out by road, and she scrounged some food to feed other friends who arrived back in Rangoon from various places.

'... *Most houses in Rangoon were now unoccupied and much property had been left behind. I should be off myself soon I supposed, and should have to fill the car with tins of petrol and leave my two hundred books behind...'* Three days later she saw two colleagues off on a ship for England. Then there was a Government order that all civilian cars had to be out of Rangoon within twenty four hours or destroyed. So they had to go.

One of her older brothers, Melrose was a Lt. Colonel in the Indian Army, and he sent her a coded message warning that the main route through Toungoo was unsafe. This meant they would have to go the longer way westward through Prome.

There was the chaos of preparations to start the journey, and some problems. At the last minute some Indians appeared - '.. *Couldn't we take them? And their wives and children and grandparents and aunts and half-brothers and third cousins - about thirty in all?*

There was Canon Harding and his driver and luggage in one car; a Burmese Driver and a Cathedral worker in Donald Moxon's car – he himself had joined the troops at Pegu. Hugh Wilson and Evelyn Websper in another car. And Josephine in a fourth car '...*plus a multitude of tins of petrol...'* Somebody had an idea. They would loot the Mission to Seamen's bus which was known to be in their garage and John Matthew would drive it. At 4.30 pm that day they left Rangoon. Others she knew also left around this time, including the Dufferin hospital staff.

There were problems right from the beginning of the journey. Twenty miles out of Rangoon the bus had a puncture, and the key to the lock of the spare wheel was probably back in Rangoon in the Mission to Seamen's garage. Some went back to search for it, and some cars went on and arrived after dark at a P.W.D.(Public Works Dept.) bungalow which was already full of people. '... *We decided to make it fuller, for driving on strange roads in the black-out was not much fun. The bus and the last car arrived at midnight...* '

The next day the bus broke down twelve miles from Prome. Josephine described their attempts to get it going, and later a trip to Prome to find a mechanic. Members of the group went in various directions, with most of them going on to Allanmyo.

So far she was travelling with other colleagues, but there seemed to be some anxiety within the group, with some people getting impatient and moving on before the others. There didn't seem to be a clear plan of what lay ahead. On February 22nd they went on to Magwe where the Commissioner's wife gave them tea, but they were not allowed to stay, there was an aerodrome nearby and the place was crowded. They travelled on to Yenangyaung where the ancient oilfields were.

Later these had to be destroyed by the Allies. The Japanese were advancing in this direction and the battle in this area happened around April 11th. The oil fields and refinery were blown up to prevent them falling into the hands of the Japanese, and this difficult and dangerous task was done on April 16th.

The landscape was dominated by the huge clouds of black smoke, and some British troops were encircled by Japanese soldiers. Chinese soldiers aided the escape of Allied soldiers, who lost equipment and were forced to begin the long retreat towards India through increasingly inaccessibly countryside. There were wounded men short of water and struggling on foot in the intense heat of the dry season.

Three weeks before this happened Josephine's group had two days of rest in a deserted parsonage in Yenangyaung, with a few hours of comfort and a walk to the Club in the evening. On the 24th there was an early service in Yenangyaung church and then they set out again in three cars, having left the bus in Prome. Various members of the party went on ahead, including George Appleton .

George Appleton appears later in Dr Russell's story. He and his wife were to create a convalescent home for sick and injured soldiers in Maymyo which sadly soon had to be moved on, with many unfit soldiers eventually having to start the walk out of Burma in April and May.

There were other difficulties on this the first part of Josephine's journey. The roads were rough and they spent one day crossing the dry sandy beds of about thirteen small rivers, with a car getting stuck, and two cars needing to be unloaded. '…. *We passed Myingyan, the dustiest place in Burma, and spent the night in a remote P.W.D. bungalow fifty miles from Mandalay.'*

21

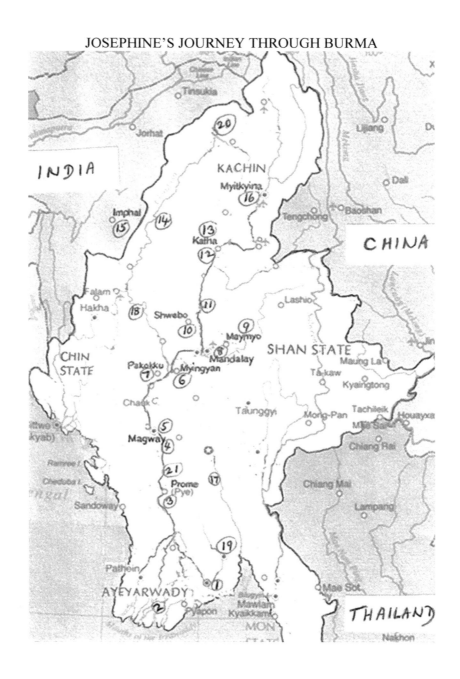

FEBRUARY

1 Rangoon (Yangon)

2 (Ayeyarwady) Irrawaddy Delta villages such as Shwelaung, Chaungwa and Nyaungngu

3 Prome (Pye)

4 Magwe

5 Yenaungyaung

6 Myingyan

7 Pakokku

8 Mandalay

9 Maymyo

10 Shwebo

11 Mogok

12 Katha

13 Indaw

14 Homalin

15 Imphal in India

16 Myitkyina – strategic airfield taken by the Japanese on May 8th 1942

17 Toungoo

18 Kalewa

19 Pegu (Bago)

20 Shingbwigang *'Nov. 2nd All Souls' Day.(1942)…We waited four and a half months hearing rumours and scraps of news now and then. Two thousand people were held up in the Hukawng valley at a place called Shingbwigang, on the other side of a river unfordable in the rains. The track too was knee-deep in mud…'* Josephine

21 The great Irrawaddy River which flows south from the Himalayas.

CHAPTER 4
February/ March
The bombing of Mandalay

'…Burning debris was flying over into our compound and we had fifty gallons of petrol in the garage…' **Josephine**

Mandalay   (dml)

Market in Mandalay   (dml)

Josephine's group reached Mandalay on February 25th and were to experience more air raids. Josephine mentioned a number of friends, including Dorothy Lewis who she had known since college days, and who later became her sister in law in 1947. And there was Rosina Simmonds who expressed her disbelief in what was happening – '... "*I have brought so many Japanese babies into the world in this hospital,*' *she said, 'I have so many Japanese friends that I am sure they would not bomb this hospital."* However she dutifully sat in the trench every time there was a raid...'

Dorothy and her brother Christopher Lewis were looking after a woman on a stretcher who had just had a surgical operation, and they left on a boat for Kalewa on the Chindwin, the first stage of an overland road to India. Many of the military and thousands of refugees reached India on these routes which later were threatened by the Japanese advance, and made more difficult by the monsoon rains of late April and May. Josephine did not mention her plans, and possibly had not yet thought what she would do. Meanwhile March was an eventful time of more air raids, more news of evacuations and more confusion about where safety could be found.

Just over two weeks after they left Rangoon the city was taken by the Japanese on March 8th. The Allies then hoped that a front could be held south of Mandalay, together with the Chinese Expeditionary Force, but in fact the Japanese were reinforced with divisions sent from Malaya and the Dutch East Indies after the falls of Singapore and Java. Air raids were attacking almost all towns and cities in Burma and civil administration was breaking down.

Also around March 8th Chinese troops took over the defence of Toungoo but after their brave and prolonged resistance the town was taken by the Japanese around March 29th. This was eighty miles east of Prome and the place where Josephine had been warned not to travel by her brother. The capture of Toungoo opened up the way for the Japanese to advance into central Burma.

Again Josephine described the indecision around her '..*March in Mandalay was like January in Rangoon. The same question was in everybody's mind. 'Shall we go? Is it safe to stay?'* Now it was no longer possible to get to India by boat. Evacuation planes could now only fly from airfields in the north of the country, and she knew of organized walking groups going up the Chindwin. The Japanese were in Toungoo but along with many others she thought that they could not reach Mandalay before the serious rains of the monsoon. Sadly she was very soon to be proved wrong about this, and in believing that refuge could be found in the hill stations in Upper Burma. She wrote: '… *Certainly it would be safe in Mogok where the orphans from Bishop's Home and S. Matthew's School had been taken…'*

Fifteen children without parents came up the river from schools that had been closed and Josephine was drawn into making extra journeys taking them to various places – Maymyo 42 miles, Shwebo, 60 miles and Sagaing 12 miles. This took her several days. Then the British built school at Shwebo was closed

Old photo of the school at Shwebo (dml)

This meant more trips with children, one day on the river and sixty miles up the hill road in a bus. But when she arrived at Mogok people there were also preparing to leave. She came back and talked to the authorities in Mandalay and a plan was made that she should go there after Easter. But no one really knew what was going to happen.

In Mandalay she was for the moment with friends. Sacks of post had been brought up from Rangoon in which she found seventy letters for people she knew, and four from her own home. On April 3rd she was sitting in the Mission House, between the Post Office and the Telegraph Office and not far from the railway station. Suddenly with no warning there were planes overhead, and bombs started falling nearby.

THE BOMBING OF MANDALAY

They lay on the floor on their faces. Josephine and a friend went across to try and help at the hospital but they were surrounded by fire. Stretchers, lorries and ambulances took the patients off to other hospitals. With others she hurriedly helped take hospital equipment in their cars to the Winchester Mission half a mile away, together with their own property from the house, food, petrol from the garage and the weary nurses and two little Chinese twins in their cradles whose parents could not be traced.

They paused to drink tea. She returned yet again to the hospital compound and found the clergy trying to extinguish a fire in the chapel roof with no hosepipe, no pump and no ladder, only water from the well. Somehow they saved the roof. Padre Garrad who had worked in Burma for many years returned to the Winchester Mission to find his house full, as were the school buildings in the compound, with people from the bombed parts of the town, Indians, Chinese and Anglo-Burmese. They wanted rice and salt and pots to cook with.

There was the problem of water supplies – would there be enough in the well in the compound? Many had nowhere to sleep. And there would be twelve of them for a meal in the mission house that evening instead of three. She thought of the feeding of the five thousand – '...*we ended Good Friday with prayers in Christchurch. We went back to our own house to sleep for the fire had died down in the immediate neighbourhood...*'

The next day parts of Mandalay were still burning. They tried to clean up the hospital and St Mary's church which was partly damaged. An evacuee camp was organized tens miles out of town on the Maymyo road.

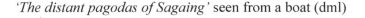

'The distant pagodas of Sagaing' seen from a boat (dml)

On Easter Day Josephine travelled to Sagaing with Padre Garrad where he took a service for twelve people. As they came out of the confusion and noise of Mandalay to the peace of Sagaing he told her it made him feel '...*like the disciples who found their Lord at Emmaeus... I was glad he had come away from it for an hour or two, and I hoped he was taking courage from the Great Failure of Good Friday when he saw the place where he had worked for over thirty years fast being destroyed and his flock scattered hither and thither...'* About four weeks later Sagaing was to suffer heavy air raids.

Over the next few days parts of Mandalay continued to burn. Bazaars and shops were closed and there were fewer and fewer people left. There was much looting, Chinese troops marched in on April 6th and a curfew was enforced. On the 8th there was another air raid. She described fires raging around the Winchester Mission compound, and their cars *'began running up and down again'* taking everything the other way. There was a wall of fire on three sides of the compound with flames curling round the trees through the bare branches and over the roofs of the wooden buildings, with a strong breeze blowing.

A frantic effort was made to pull down some of the wooden buildings to save the Church and the Mission House. The breeze carried the sparks across the treetops and a tree was on fire, though they managed to beat it out in time. '... *Every time I drove into the compound the fire was nearer.* It was feared the church would catch fire, and she took a sack of rice and many other things and broke the springs of the car.

The Mission compound was saved while whole areas around were reduced to ashes. The fire died down and some people could sleep in their own houses that night, while the already full compound sheltered more people than before.

On April 9th she wrote that they had so much property in their house and the compound outside that she and Rosina Simmonds were given a military guard at night. This was a relief as the raids continued. They could sometimes hear shooting which was probably the Chinese guard dealing with night looters.

At 2 o'clock in the morning of April 10th the brewery was on fire and the flames were very high. '... *Burning debris was flying over into our compound and we had fifty gallons of petrol in the garage. I put as much as I dared into the car with the broken spring and asking one of the soldiers to come with me because of the curfew, I took it down to the Winchester Mission. I wondered how many more times the property was to go to and fro between the two compounds. The brewery fire cast a dull red glow all around, queer and uncanny it all felt…'*

Later that day she found Padre Garrad sweeping his compound and he took her to see a sick Chinese woman sheltering in the school with her seven children. They thought she had cholera and Hugh Wilson took her off to the hospital. '…*Padre Garrad gave me his last tin of Klim to feed the baby not yet weaned…'*

The next day Josephine helped Rosina Simmonds and her nurses to pack as they were planning to go to Mohnyin, the BCMS headquarters on the 14th, and Padre Garrad was to go with them. He was soon to get a place on an evacuation plane, as did some of Josephine's colleagues.

Dr Russell's account is about to begin – he was a surgeon working for the BCMS at the hospital in Mohnyin. He and his wife had stayed on, hearing news of the war but hoping they would not have to leave. At this time evacuation staff were on their way to take over Myitkyina airfield and the first planes carrying refugees soon left from there.

Scenes of great hope and desperation were to unfold at this tiny airfield in the remote town which was to become the last place where planes could fly refugees out of Burma. And this vital operation was only going to be able to continue for a few weeks.

CHAPTER FIVE
April

'...Little though they knew it, never again would we as a family walk along that peaceful river bank...' **Dr Stanley Farrant Russell**

Dr Russell wrote: *The day had proved more than ordinarily peaceful. On a busy mission station, such as Mohnyin, Sunday is often far from a day of rest, but the 12th April 1942 had lived up to its name. As the deep gong boomed its call to worship in the morning, the brightly-clad congregation gathered in the cool church, thus early before the heat of midday made attention difficult. To the Burmese service as they were wont, went the doctor's three eldest children, Margaret, Rosemary and little Paul. Baby Priscilla played in her pen on the veranda of the bungalow near at hand. The last hymn sung, the church soon emptied and the worshippers scattered to their morning meal.*

In spite of the mounting temperature after breakfast, the little family left the doctor's bungalow for its weekly enjoyable walk down to the river, now sadly shrunk by weeks of drought. Along the sandy banks comely village women industriously thumped their piles of washing, while naked brown children scampered in and out of the sparkling water.

A village scene   (sfr)

A slow-moving bullock cart lumbered across the lofty wooden bridge, around the piles of which the stream chuckled and gurgled. In the

distance, a hpongyi, his robe an orange flame, stroke down the bank, his little acolyte at his heels. Behind its screen of lofty trees on which the paddy birds showed white against the blue sky, the monastery made known the hour with boom of gong and thud of drum. Little though they knew it, never again would we as a family walk along that peaceful river bank.

The day wore away. The sun sank in the west, hidden at last behind the distant hills which stood out clear-cut against the darkening sky. The children went to their beds. The English service was over. Muriel and I sat quietly reading in our book-lined study. Nearly three weeks had passed since the majority of the women and children of the Mission had been evacuated by air from Shwebo, two hundred miles to the South, to the safety of India.

...Daily the wave of Japanese invasion advanced up the map of Burma, submerging that once happy land in misery and blood. But more than four hundred miles still lay between the cruel invaders and the peaceful scene of our story. An Allied army surely barred the way. There was every hope that the advance would be halted until the monsoon should make campaigning impossible.

But then they received a telegram on the Sunday evening: *'...From Deputy Commissioner Myitkyina stop cannot agree to family remaining longer Mohnyin stop please proceed Myitkyina for evacuation India sixteenth without fail stop.'*

Muriel was forced to start packing for an uncertain journey with four young children and another due in four months' time.

....In normal times, the up mail train reached Mohnyin at nine each morning, and was due to arrive at the northern terminus some six hours later. But for days past, long and crowded trains of frightened refugees from the war-stricken south had passed through at irregular intervals. Enquiry at the station could settle no doubts. That day's train could not arrive before the afternoon at the earliest. When it should draw in there was little likelihood of any more would-be passengers being able to force their way into already over-full carriages or trucks. And should the train reach Mohnyin during the night, the task would be more hopeless still.

The family and their friends found an empty goods-wagon standing unused at the station and prepared it for their use, but as the day wore on no train arrived. At 1 a.m the following morning there was a message that the train was finally expected and the family roused itself. *'...Picture the little procession wending its way to the station beneath the stars.*

Wide-eyed children, Priscilla in her pram, the devoted Nanny, Ma Kin, soon to be bereft of the charges she loved, nurses from the hospital come to say farewell, other friends, and the lamps casting flickering shadows around... ...the last words were said, the last lamp flickered away into the distance and the wagon door was slammed to. The children were put down on the camp beds and soon dropped off again, as peacefully as if they were still at home....'

The family waited in their goods-wagon and finally the train arrived after five o'clock *'...a tremendous train laden with fugitives of many races, in every variety of truck or carriage, their pitiful possessions piled around them.'* The goods-wagon was coupled to the train and Dr Russell travelled with his family. *'....Through the long hours the refugee train crept and panted on towards the north. Station after little station dropped behind, each with its small crowd of staring villagers. Not even the oldest man had ever seen such happenings – a whole country fleeing from the invader!*

Orders came through from the D.C. at Myitkyina that all refugees were to leave the train at Sahmaw, (a little town housing a sugar factory) as Myitkyina was crowded, with no accommodation and a shortage of food. To the Russell family this presented the prospect of a very real fear of being stranded in Sahmaw. However, while they were still on the train and discussing what to do, it started up again and they were moved on. *'...Through thick jungle ran the line over little booming bridges, under the shadow of steep hills, on which stood small Jinghpaw villages, their long huts surrounded by dry, burnt clearings. For miles the great Pidaung Game Reserve lay on each side of the track, but no wandering herd of elephants or buffaloes could be seen. Then all sign of human habitation disappeared and the train rumbled slowly on through the long hot afternoon.*

Myitkyina drew near. Huts and houses began to show in the thinning jungle. There came a distant hum, growing rapidly louder, and a ponderous twin-engined plane swept low over the trees, and sped away to the west. At this sign of contact with the outside world and its promise of escape many a heart on the crowded train must have beaten quicker.

It was after three o'clock before the engine clattered and swayed across the points and finally stopped in Myitkyina. On a siding beyond the station stood, disconsolately in a row, a dozen mighty engines. A brief time before in all their glory of green paint and gleaming brass, they had thundered north from Rangoon at the head of the Mandalay mail-trains.

APRIL

It had been the fastest metre-gauge engines in the world!   Behind them had travelled Governors, globe-trotters, multitudes, distinguished and otherwise on their lawful occasions.   Now the engines stood helpless, immobilized by the removal of the connecting-rods, fittings and valves, their sides already rusty and tarnished.   Three weeks later they were in Japanese hands.

Old photo of train in Burma   (sfr)

In normal times a very pleasant little town, Myitkyina stands at the northern end of the railway line from Rangoon, some 700 miles away, and on a big bend of the Irrawaddy river. Its very name means in Burmese "Near the Big River" and here a mighty flood half-a-mile wide swings from the tangled hills of Northern Burma which give it birth, down on its thousand-mile journey to the sea.

STORIES OF SURVIVAL IN BURMA

The Irrawaddy river at Myitkyina   (dml)

Surrounded by smooth lawns, the bungalows of the Deputy Commissioner, Civil Surgeon, Policeman, Engineer and the other officials who represent the British Raj in such an outpost of Empire, stood on the high bank of the Irrawaddy.   A hospital, barracks, the usual polo-ground and golf-course made up the little settlement.

It is, or rather was, one of the more picturesque towns of a picturesque land, for in its crowded bazaar might be found members of half-a-dozen outlandish races, mingling with the more ordinary Gurkhas, Chinese, or Kachins.   Lisu, Nung, Naga or Tibetan would jostle Shan from Hkamti Long, or Yunnanese from Tengyueh.   Its merchants dealt in teak, rice, sugar-cane or jade.   Less conspicuously smuggled opium changed owners in the furtive looking huts off the main street.

...At the southern end of the mile-long crescent of river bank stood the bungalow and school of the American Baptist Mission in a large compound.   After the departure of the missionaries the whole establishment had been taken over as the Evacuee Camp – a purpose for which it was well fitted.   Its normal population expanded suddenly from the usual 150 to nearly ten times that number........Many of these bewildered evacuees often possessing nothing beyond their clothes, poured into Myitkyina from the south, paused a day or two and were then flown out into India across the hills.....the main compound lay behind a high bund or embankment;   beyond that lay a stretch of rough grass, a

steep boulder-strewn beach and the river.

All through the day a long line of refugees fringed the water's edge, bathing, washing their few poor garments or getting water for cooking......Across the wide sweep of the river lay a tangled jungle of low scrub. In the distance rose range after range of blue hills, dominated by the towering sugar-loaf peak of Seniku. At night behind those hills the lightning flickered and the thunder rumbled, forerunners of the monsoon that would soon flood the whole countryside, effectively putting a stop to all active campaigning.

...It was cheering to learn that some 700 people had been carried to Assam that day by the transport planes that swooped down on the jungle aerodrome five miles away, picked up their complement of anxious passengers and swept away to the west.....In the light of what the future revealed, it was pathetic and ominous to hear an official refusing a permit to fly to an elderly Anglo-Indian man on the ground that he was able –bodied enough to walk to Assam. There were, so the official said, tea-shops every few miles all the way! He knew little enough of the two hundred miles of jungle and grim mountain, or ravening river and engulfing mud which were to bring so many unfortunates to their death.

With hundreds of others the family now waited in the heat for many hours for a plane. The refugees of various races who were fleeing in Burma had a firm expectation that if they did manage to reach India there would be comparative safety there under the British administration.

Far from the travellers' minds would have been the many problems in India, such as riots, inflation and a devastating shortage of food for millions. Anticipating invasion of India, the Army confiscated boats, motor vehicles, carts and elephants in Bengal. This affected fishing and the moving of goods to markets. Local administration was disrupted. Food prices rose because of famine which had several causes and traders and craftsmen suffered loss of income when many people were struggling just to survive. Many men joined the Army leaving families to fend for themselves.

Aid from abroad if there was any could not approach India by the usual route because the Japanese dominated the Bay of Bengal with their navy and air force. Railways in India were overloaded with men and supplies being sent to war zones.

The British administration had involved India in the war without reference to the views of the largest political party, the Indian National Congress. In August 1942' The Quit India Act' was a civil disobedience movement in Bengal and Bihar demanding what Gandhi described as *'an orderly British withdrawal'* from India.

Within hours of Gandhi's speech tens of thousands of people including the INC leaders were imprisoned without trial by the British authorities, and many remained there for the rest of the war though Gandhi himself was released in 1944 due to ill health. Civil rights and the freedom of the press were suppressed, and the question of independence was deferred until after the war.

However the Indian Army grew to over 2 million volunteers who fought with skill and valour in the North and East African Campaign, the Western Desert Campaign and Italian Campaign, and later in Singapore and Hong Kong. The Muslim League supported the war effort and the assistance of India with its production of armaments and large donations from Indian princes was a large part of the campaign against Nazi Germany and the Imperial Empire of Japan.

Old photo of India   (dml)

APRIL

Further north in Burma Captain Gribble was to hear about the bombing of Mandalay and the breakdown of law and order. Many questions in his mind remained unanswered. He was about to travel back home from another trip into the jungle. Heavy demands were being made upon him to organize the building of the road and impose on the local people during their busy season of cultivation.

'...*The time soon arrived for our return to Headquarters. We enjoyed better luck on the return journey and with the help of the villagers here and there, successfully overcame all obstacles along the track and were able to reach Kamaing before nightfull accomplishing a journey of 104 miles in nine hours. I quickly learned, however, that there would be little or no rest.*

Orders had come through to get busy and convert the mule track to the Hukawng into a road to take cars and lorries. I was to choose sites and arrange for the building of food stores every ten or fifteen miles along 150 miles of track, to enable rice supplies to be circulated ready for the countless numbers of coolies expected to arrive within twenty days for the purpose of constructing a main highway. I was to use my influence with the tribes people inhabiting the jungle along the route for the provision of local labour. A junior officer would be sent to assist me.

What a task! My hair stood on end at the thought of it. The villagers were still grumbling because they had been called upon to construct the mule track at the beginning of the dry season. It interfered with their cultivation: could they be rallied a second time? I would have to go and meet the Chiefs and their subordinates once again and see what could be done.

I was without authentic news about the process of the war in Burma but evidently the situation was getting desperate. Slowly but surely Japanese bombers were extending their bombing raids to towns nearer and nearer to the northernmost district in Burma. At my little fishing village one could see allied transport planes passing overhead every day. It was rumoured that all women and children were being evacuated by air. Mandalay had been heavily bombed and was in ruins. Civil administration south of Mandalay had ceased. All these rumours were buzzing in my ears as I set out for yet a third time to the Valley of the Hukawng.

This hurried journeying to and fro was very disturbing and I often experienced periods of considerable anxiety. I asked myself many questions. Could we hold Upper Burma during the coming rains against the Japs? Could the Chinese armies in their new terrain in Burma score a resounding victory over their enemy at long last? In what respect was this new road intended to assist the war effort? How long would the road take to build assuming that sufficient labour would come? Soon the rains would break and the rivers become torrents and the jungle paths would turn into streams. In the low-lying jungles round the Hukawng the water would lie deep and wide. Suppose the Allies were defeated! In my ignorance of the situation I could only half appreciate the significance of what was happening – and might happen.

I was absent from Headquarters for nine days but in that short space of time over 500 members of the tribes with whom I was acquainted responded to the call, and were organized and distributed. Now they were working like ants, felling trees, building bridges, erecting bamboo sheds, and constructing rafts for use at river crossings where bridges were impossible.

At headquarters I tried to suppress some of the more fantastic rumours. After the bombing of Rangoon and many other places by Japanese Aircraft the local bazaars buzzed with rumours. One was to the effect the Germans had occupied Rangoon. This and other rumours were having a demoralizing effect on the population, and many villagers were openly discussing their coming flight to distant places of safety. Some hooligans, I had reason to believe, were planning to loot the Indian and Chinese shops and were storing large quantities of knives and spears in some caves in jungle places.

The upheaval had come at the time of the year when the grassy hillsides were being burned as a preliminary to cultivation. One night I stood at the door of my house which overlooked the surrounding country and watched the outline of flames in various directions. The dome of heaven was splashed with a bloody glare as one burst of flame succeeded another. The night seemed to emphasise the feeling of universal unease. The very air seemed affected

I thought I would walk across the brow of the hill and have a talk with my one and only white neighbour in this little town. The Missionary Padre was not at home. Wilfred Crittle had gone to see his wife to India by air. I felt lonely and distraught. I could not sit still, so I decided to go once more into the jungle to see how the Kachin villagers were tackling the job of making a mule track look like a motor road. I would not take my mules but would use a bus owned by a Burman. He was not willing to go and it was perforce necessary to commander the bus and drive it myself.

CHAPTER SIX
April

… I was really and truly afraid that night, for the school children waiting on the jetty at Thabeitkyin and for myself…' **Josephine**

Josephine was still in Mandalay. Some of her friends had left for Mohnyin. She was to do more travelling to and fro and efforts were still being made by the Evacuation authorities to get children to safety. On April 13th she went to Mogok, the area of ruby mines, on a steamer that was evacuating the European and Indian staff of the Imperial Bank, and she was told to wait there till she received a telegram about what was happening. But communications were gradually breaking down.

Progress was maddeningly slow, it took three days to do a twelve hour journey during which time an Indian woman died on board. It may have been cholera, but they weren't sure. Josephine arrived at Thabeitkyin the river port at 6 o'clock one evening and was lucky to find a bus going up the hill that day, and she arrived in Mogok at one in the morning. She met with Miss Lillian Bald and Padre John Derry and they discussed the arrangements.

Around April 17th they spent time weighing children's luggage, not knowing the tragedy which was to happen to them at Myitkyina airfield. They also spent time selling school property and stores, holding a jumble sale and getting fifty children inoculated against cholera.

'… I escaped for a walk in the hills once or twice, and the little church nearby was a peaceful refuge in the early mornings. Having just come from Mandalay I found it pleasantly cool too. I met one of the children loitering on the path way one day searching for something. 'I am looking for rubies,' he explained in all seriousness when I enquired, 'I can take them with me on the aeroplane, they will not be heavy…''

In Kamaing, Captain Gribble's neighbour, Wilfred Crittle wrote: *'For the next ten days life went on almost normally except that there was no news about anything. Newspapers, of course, had ceased functioning long before when Rangoon fell, and I had no radio so I was dependent on what I could pick up on other people's wirelesses. Actually the news was all very vague and it was difficult to say where anyone was, even the Japanese….No-one who did not experience it could have any idea of the complete chaos of communication during the last few weeks in Burma….'*

Dr Russell's wife Muriel and the children had been having a long wait for the plane at Myitkyina. . *'....Throughout that seemingly interminable day, Saturday 18th April anxious eyes scanned the sky, ears were continually listening for the hum of planes, but rarely were they satisfied. There was great congestion, it was said, over in Assam at the other end of the airline, owing to the large number of passengers the day before. Besides there had been torrential rain, and the conditions made flying difficult.*

Several lorry-loads of would-be travellers were taken to the aerodrome, and waited there for long hours, vainly hoping for a flight. But in the late afternoon, most of them were brought back, tired, hot, thirsty and sadly depressed....'

The family passed the time as best they could, meeting old friends, watching the children climbing an old guava tree and strolling along the river bank. Another night passed. ... *In spite of the hardness of the boards, the little ones slept soundly. Not even the sudden thunderstorm which swept across hills and river in the small hours disturbed them. Blazing lightning illuminated the wild scene, the rain fell in sheets, the wind drove in savage gusts over the veranda. At last the storm passed; the thunder rumbled away in the distance. The great river flowed silently past the sleeping camp.*

The next morning brought the promise of great heat after the night's storm. All eyes in the camp turned upwards at the hum of a plane. It was high in the sky and the experts took a gloomy delight in pronouncing it a Jap reconnaissance plane, sent to spy out the situation and perhaps herald the coming of the dreaded bombers....But it was not only the enemy that flew over that anxious town on Sunday, 19th April. One after the other the big transport Douglas DC-3 planes winged their way from the east, from China and Lashio, swooped down for a few moments on the baked airfield to fill up with refugees and rising, sped away to safety in the west...... "How long would it be before I would hear those beloved voices again, asking God to bless Daddy, Mummy, Margaret and Rosemary, Paul and Priscilla?" I was filled with inexpressible sadness at the thought of our impending parting.

...Each plane carried at least fifty people with their possessions. According to regulations in the heat of mid-day the total load was not to exceed 5,000 lbs. But again and again the total load was nearer 6,500 lbs and those who watched the take-off heaved sighs of relief as the aircraft became air-borne and rose above the surrounding jungle.....The self-starters whined, then one mighty engine burst into ear-shattering

life; the other followed.   They quickened into thunder as the huge plane turned into the wind and began to move down the field.   A billowing cloud of dust rose, hiding everything from the watchers.   The roar of the engines died to an all-pervading hum;   the dust settled and there was the plane, rapidly fading to a dot above the western hills.

Those of us that were left behind in our private grief walked slowly and silently back towards the waiting cars for the jouney back to Mohnyin.

Josephine and her group and fifty children were waiting at Mogok.. Like Captain Gribble she mentioned the great fires on the hillsides. On April 21st a telegram arrived, space was reserved on the 'Minthamee' on the 22nd. The D.S.P, arranged buses to take them the 60 miles to the river port. They left Mogok in four buses at 3 a.m.   The night was dark with no moon, and though they were tightly packed with children and luggage it was chilly and the air was fresh.

'...*The forest fires were a wonderful sight; rings of fire on the wooded hillsides above us and below as we sped down the winding road.   This was the time of the year when the jungle folk cleared and prepared fresh land for cultivation in the coming season. Then came the grey dawn and a chilly breeze;   and the sunrise and the day; and the cluster of Burmese houses which was Thabeitkyin and the river.   We had ninety minutes to wait on the jetty and then our boat would come...*'

The boat arrived at 5 p.m. and stopped only to tell them there was no room. The space reserved for their group had been taken at the last minute by the hospital authorities in Mandalay, and the boat was crowded with stretcher cases.

The children were disappointed and tired, and the adults were very worried, as all the boats arriving from Mandalay would be crowded and telegraphic communication with the authorities was now no longer possible. They had something to eat and the children unrolled their bedding on the covered jetty.

It must have been very difficult to know what to do next. They decided that the school party must camp there for a few days and John Derry and Josephine were to go back by road through the Shan States to Mandalay. They would go by bus to Mogok to collect John's car from his brother's house and travel all night. '...*We arrived in Mogok at 11 p.m. and Mrs Derry gave us a meal.   But it was windy and wet, and deciding   it   was folly to attempt a narrow rough hill road in weather such as this, we slept for a few hours. April 23rd 6 a.m. We set out, John Derry, his brother Dick and I. It was cold here in the hills after the storm. They drove in turn and I slept now and then in the back of the car. The Shan States are beautiful and ideal for a touring holiday. We ate Indian food at dirty little wayside shops and thoroughly appreciated it. At one point the Japanese were not very far from the road, but fortunately we did not know then and we saw few people and little traffic until we came near Maymyo. I saw the Gokteik gorge and the bridge for the last time. It was destroyed a few days later.*

Josephine was mistaken here, but it is interesting that she made this comment. The spectacular Gokteik viaduct was a link on the Rangoon – Lashio route to the Burma Road, and despite some debate within the military command it was not blown up either in 1942 or later in the Burma Campaign. The Japanese took control of it undamaged.

The viaduct is between Maymyo and Lashio, and at the time was the highest bridge in Burma and the largest railway trestle in the world, built in 1900 with parts shipped from America. It was 2260 feet long and 320 feet high across the deep Gokteik gorge near Nawnghkio.

Old photo of Gokteik viaduct   (sfr)

APRIL

They reached Maymyo that evening. The Parsonage was closed and it seemed like all her colleagues had left, but they found George Appleton and George Tidey in the Military Convalescent Home preparing to go in a day or two. They were shocked to see John and Josephine. It was too late to go on to Mandalay and they slept in Maymyo.

Old photo of street in Maymyo   (dml)

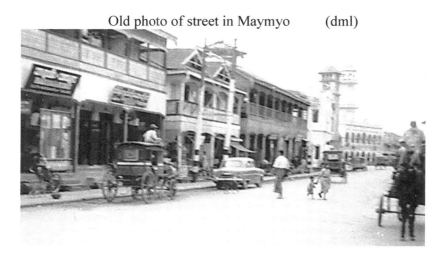

When George Appleton and his wife had arrived in Maymyo, having had to leave Rangoon, they had created a convalescent home for injured soldiers which became a British Military Hospital.   However as the war drew closer the convalescent unit was told to move northwards to Mohnyin. There was still hope at this stage that the Japanese would not reach Mohnyin.

The unit left on a train which was seventeen hours late. There was a story of Evelyn Websper delivering a baby on the train. (Josephine knew Evelyn who cared for mothers and babies in the Irrawaddy Delta). There was a long train journey lasting for days during which time injured men had little food or water in the intense heat. When they reached Mohnyin their stay was to be for a short time only and some who were not flown out on planes had to begin the walk to India in Dr Russell's party.

Josephine wrote: '... *I was really and truly afraid that night, for the school children waiting on the jetty at Thabeitkyin and for myself...* ' On April 24th she and John Derry went down to Mandalay which was in ruins and still burming in places. There had just been another air raid. ' ... *I found the Evacuation Officer preparing himself to go north and he was very upset to see me. 'I thought you would all be well on the way to India by now,' he said. 'I reserved space on the boat and in fact went down myself to see it roped off.' We went down to the foreshore three miles away. In every direction there was nothing to be seen but ashes and debris and burnt out buildings. The Agricultural College was still standing, and the fort with the European houses east of it and the Queen Alexandra's Children's Hospital and the Winchester Mission. That was Mandalay when I left it. It was deserted too except for the Chinese troops and a few European officials.*

We found that another boat was due to leave that evening, a cargo boat being used for evacuees with just one long open deck and no accommodation for passengers. We roped off a place in front, and this time John Derry and I were there to keep other folk out! At 5 pm they were loading fuel when there was a sudden wind storm on the Irrawaddy, a common occurrence at this time of the year. On Mandalay foreshore that meant a sandstorm too.....we should not be able to leave until Saturday morning.

Old photo of boats on the river   (dml)

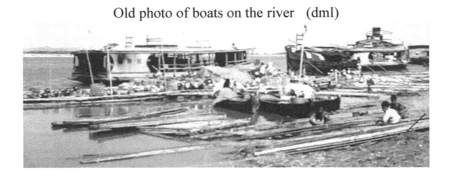

April 25th   The boat was crowded with Indians and Anglo-Burmans. Some had no room to lie down .... wouldn't we let them use our reserved space for the time being? But how should we get them out when our children came on board at Thabeitkyin? I was firm.....so selfish she is ....a Christian missionary too...'

This was to be a frightening and frustrating experience. To start with, Josephine was worried because there was no sign of the boat leaving. There were often air raids at ten 'o'clock and it was dangerous to be near the railway or the jetty. She was surprised at how nervous she was becoming and told herself that God would help. They started at nine o'clock with a loaded flat attached each side and travelled very slowly at about two or three miles an hour. There were people walking along the river bank faster than the boat was travelling. Twice they stopped to load more wood and tied up at 6 pm with Mandalay Hill still in sight. When it got dark they could see flames of fires still burning.

Stranded on a boat in the remote countryside Josephine couldn't have known that around this time General Alexander made the difficult decision to withdraw all British and Allied forces to India.

The Indian captain said he wanted space to load more wood on board. He filled the space reserved for the children with Indian evacuees and said some of them would be getting off at the Indian camp below Thabeitkyin, though some of them denied this. She felt helpless but tried to take strength from her faith.

The days passed slowly, with many people having to sleep on the crowded boat. Josephine found a way of making the journey more bearable. Despite all the coming and going she still had her luggage with her. '*...April 27th   I sat up where I had been lying down, and while it was still dark and my Indian companions around me still slept, I stepped over their bodies and went downstairs to wash.   I had a brilliant idea.   I would sit on the roof until the sun was hot.   It was clean and there was fresh air and alone-ness, though next time I should bring my blanket for corrugated iron was not very comfortable to sit on.   Three hours here in the morning and two in the evening would make the journey more tolerable.   I had a number of books too from the Mogok club marked 'not to be taken away.' That night it poured with rain and the deck was drenched.   We crowded even more closely together away from the open sides of the boat...*'

The next day they were still far away from Thabeitkyin, but they arrived at the Indian camp at Kyaukmyaung.   Some Indians did get off and she and John were able to clear the space and sweep it in readiness for the children. Japanese planes went over and they heard air raids in Shwebo, seventeen miles away. They were still travelling very slowly.

'*...April 29th   We loaded wood again for two hours.   Other boats had been passing us and folk began to complain.   The Indian captain, it was said, had had orders to return to Mandalay after this trip.   He wanted to delay so that there would not be time – and there was not, for the Japanese were in Mandalay very soon after.   The captain was making money too from his load of evacuees, charging two annas for a jug of hot water and selling the free rations.   The slower our progress,*

*the better for him.   1 pm   We reached Thabeitkyin, four and a half days
for a twelve hour journey.*

*The school party had gone, but there was a message from Lillian Bald;
'we have waited so long and suppose you cannot get any
accommodation. I got a message through to the District Commissioner in
Katha and he has sent his own launch down to fetch us.   We left at 9 am
today.   Perhaps you will not be far behind and we shall see you again.'
I was now four hours behind them and at the rate we were going, I should
be two days behind when we reached Katha.   Such a futile effort on my
part, but I was glad they had got away and they would certainly be
travelling in more comfort.*

They never did meet again. In George Tidey's diary he recorded a letter
later written by Miss Bald of the Bishop's Home Orphanage. Tragically
soon after writing this letter from the Hukawng valley she was to lose her
life, together with family members, other adults and about thirty
children. This heartbreaking letter recorded how far they had travelled
and that they were about 100 miles from the railway in India. They were
starving, sick, exhausted, soaking wet and surrounded by
corpses.....Josephine did not yet know what was to happen, and how her
own life was to become extremely uncertain.

*April 30th   The boat did not move at all.   Four Burmese women coolies
spent the morning loading nine tons of wood.   At noon we were going
downstream 200 yards to load nine tons more, we were told.   We should
not get an inch nearer to Katha that day.   Somebody started a campaign
for volunteers to load the wood, by making a chain of about fifty people
up the bank from the boat to the stack of wood. We passed it down a log
at a time   The job was finished in two hours and the captain very
annoyed, went on a few miles.*

On April 30th 27 Japanese bombers flew towards the Ava bridge and
heavily bombed the village of Sagaing at the northern end where
Josephine had accompanied Padre Garrad in early April.   The Ava
Bridge across the Irrawaddy had been built in 1934 and was almost three
quarters of a mile long.It was an enormous structure carrying a double
rail track and a road on each side. On the night of the 30th the British
blew up one span of the bridge and damaged another. This was another
sad moment when they were forced to destroy part of the intrastructure of
Burma they had built.

Old photo of the Ava-Sagaing Bridge   (dml)

CHAPTER 7
April/May

'…Events move so fast that I know not what the next day will bring…'
Captain Gribble

In late April Captain Gribble had gone back into the jungle once again to oversee the work preparing to build the road. '*…It was a relief to be back in the jungle villages again away from the scares, rumours and troubles that beset one in the towns. Each place seemed to have its peculiar charm. It was pleasant to sit in the cool near a river and watch the women carry their water pots down to the bank and fill them. It was pleasant to wander along the track soon after dawn and take a shot at jungle fowl or pheasant. I recall my delight at finding a new species of tree orchid. A deer would be disturbed and go bounding away through the undergrowth and I would arrive in camp to find some new matter to be dealt with, perhaps Kachins wanting to get instructions about the road work , or asking for medicine.*

…That night we experienced a storm of wind and rain. As usual at this time of the year the storm opened with a waving flash of green light that filled the horizon and showed up each leaf and twig and bough in black relief. A distant crash followed the illumination. Then gusts of wind. Gradually the storm approached and then just as the brilliant flashes of lightning and noise seemed to meet overhead the rain came.

And such rain! It tumbled down in a stream with all the frustrated energy of a season of dryness…..

…While returning to camp one evening after a strenuous day inspecting work done by the Kachins I began to ponder afresh on the situation in Burma. The news was getting unbelievably critical. Yet here in this part all was so peaceful. It had been a lovely sunny day and the forest was at its best. The trees were a symphony in green, a dark hem in the undergrowth and passing through every variety of shade as it rose towards the pale green of the tree tops. ….That night I meant to leave my portable radio alone. On second thoughts I decided to tune in. After all it was my only means in the jungle of keeping in touch with events that were very far from normal. I learned from the radio that the situation in Burma was deteriorating rapidly. The Shan States (in the east) *were overrun by the enemy. The news left me in grave doubts about the future. The Labour Corps would be cut off and never able to reach the scene of the proposed new road.*

Once more I hurried back to Headquarters arriving there on the 30th April 1942. The bazaar was seething with excitement; parties of refugees fleeing from Central Burma had found their way to this quiet little fishing village, bringing with them stories of bombings and atrocities committed by Japanese troops. Conditions were becoming unsanitary and food was scarce. I tried to get in touch with higher authority by telephone. The line was not working. The village was becoming more and more choked with refugees and, astounding as it may seem, there was now no way of escape from Burma except through the wild country of the Hukawng valley and the tortuous mountains beyond!

Wilfred Crittle wrote: *'for the next few days I was busy telegraphing to all our stations within reach of the telegraph wire and sending runners to those who were off the beaten track. Everything was greatly complicated by considerable delays in transmission and by the fact that the telegraph line south of Mohnyin was repeatedly out of order, though whether this was by reason of accident or sabotage I did not know. It seemed to me that there was now a very real danger that our people in the Shan States might get cut off by the Japanese army advancing rapidly up the centre of Burma.'*

On May 1st Japanese troops entered the ruins of Mandalay and met no resistance. In his diary on May 1st Ted Rushton (one of Dr Russell's party) wrote that orders came through for the British Military hospital to get all patients to Myitkyina airfield, and all personnel were to get out of Burma as well as they could by making their own way. There were still planes flying out of Myitkyina until May 8th when the Japanese captured the town and airfield.

Captain Gribble wrote: *May 1ˢᵗ ....Nearly all Kachin men are the proud owners of a gun, for protection against wild animals. But this privilege with a few exceptions is not enjoyed by any one living outside the hill tracts. Every Shan-Burman villager is, however, the possessor of a long-bladed knife, a valuable and formidable weapon. Few Indians possess any sort of a weapon and rely on the protection afforded by the civil administration. Authority today looks very shaky indeed and might collapse at any moment. Events move so fast that I know not what the next day will bring. The road from the railway to Kamaing is reported to be black with refugees.........I have not received any intimidation from outside possibly because the telegraph and telephone have ceased to function. ....today I learn that the local mixed force of Burman and Kachin Police have been instructed to draw their pay and go to their homes. Thus the slender thread of authority in the town is likely to snap at any moment. Then what will happen? The Kachins have a pretty good idea of what might happen for they are hurriedly sending their women and children to villages deep in the jungle.*

A newcomer, a tall bewhiskered Sikh policeman came to see me. 'Sahib,' he said in Hindustani, 'I was lucky to escape from Rangoon when that city was evacuated. I reached Mandalay after many nights hiding and sleeping in the jungle. How I escaped with my life I do not know. From Mandalay I managed to get on a train and eventually found my way here.' He came a little closer and almost whispered, 'Sahib, I am staying in the Police Lines. You must let me and my pal guard your bungalow or....' And he drew his finger across his throat. 'Believe me I have seen many tragedies during the past few weeks.'

I smiled, thanked him and said I would send for him and his pal should I find it necessary, I had many native friends who I knew would be helpful and kind to refugees and I regarded the policeman's tale as greatly exaggerated. The next day this good man joined the stream of refugees hastening to the frontier of India.

While Josephine was held up on a slow moving boat, Dr Russell and others at Mohnyin were finally forced to think about leaving. Rev. Edgar Pearson (one of Dr Russell's party on the walk) spent some weeks in Kamaing, before returning to Mohnyin. He wrote that there was conflicting information on the radio, because the South Burma radio news suggested that the Japanese would be driven back, while the BBC World Service revealed the worsening situation.

His visit to Kamaing and Wilfred Crittle led him to comment that under British rule in Upper Burma since 1885 the government had helped protect the Kachins from Chinese invasions and had promoted peace amongst them. Thousands of Kachins had now begun to erect new buildings in Mohnyin to house the allied wounded soldiers from the Military Hospital in Maymyo, not knowing that this would not be needed for many more days.

Pearson witnessed how hard Dr Russell worked to cope with his own patients and new arrivals from Maymyo. Many soldiers were not fit enough to start an exhausting trek in rough country and later some became so ill they had to be carried on stretchers.

Dr Russell with one of his patients   (pr)

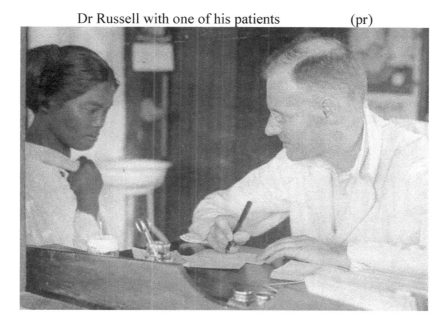

It was a time of great uncertainty and upheaval – to Dr Russell's great grief some medical and surgical instruments were stolen. When urgent news arrived that the Japanese were very close, much equipment had to be destroyed, including generators, pumps, medical gear, drugs and food stores.

Dr Russell described the arrival of the injured troops. *...There was no doubt that the tide of war was coming nearer....day by day, the long trains, crowded with homeless refugees, rumbled their slow way up to the valley, towards a possible means of escape from Myitkyina.....that afternoon, large numbers of wounded soldiers, British, Indians, Chinese, with others already convalescent, medical personnel, English nursing sisters, and much of the equipment of two military hospitals evacuated from Maymyo, had arrived in Mohnyin...*

...later a long line of bullock carts brought wounded and sick to our little hospital, from which our own patients had been hastily cleared, and filled it to overflowing. There followed a busy afternoon, doing dressings, many of them desperately bad ones, heavily maggot-infected, putting on plasters to fractured legs, preparing for amputation of a gangrenous limb, and settling in the less seriously injured.

...That Saturday afternoon, May 2nd, we who were phyically fit enough, officers and missionaries, met on a veranda to make plans for the long

journey overland, for it was obvious that our hours in Mohnyin were numbered...A train was coming up, we were told, which would carry us the forty miles to Sahmaw, the first stage on our journey to Assam; the time of its arrival was unknown, so all day long we were waiting....

.....The native Christians, with the few remaining nurses from the hospital, and the blind School from Lower Burma moved from Mohnyin out to the little village of Bilumyo, six miles from the railway-line where it was felt they would be safer.....

Old photo of Bilumyo   (dml)

He described distributing stores amongst friends before they left. *...At 2.30 am on Monday morning I was awakened from a troubled sleep by voices, and there came into my room two Army doctors, friends of mine,who had hurried up from their train while it stood in the station, to warn us to leave as soon as possible. The train service, said they,would cease to function in the course of the next few hours: that day there had been a terrible smash at the junction fifty miles to the south, half a train running down the hill back into the station, at forty miles an hour, and crashing into another heavily laden ambulance train; (some of the casualties I myself saw and treated later that morning). This nocturnal visit settled our few remaining doubts, and showed us clearly that the time had come, and we must go....'*

Captain Gribble was at home in Kamaing.   Everything was changing. *May 3rd ...from the little Mission church nearby came the slow deep booming of a Burmese gong. The sound swelled and ebbed. I had forgotten the Rev. Wilfred Crittle.   He must have returned and in all that turmoil decided to hold the usual Sunday service for Christian Kachins. I decided to walk over there.   I saw Crittle, who was wearing his surplice at the open door of the Church, where a simple but impressive scene met my eyes.   On the earthen floor knelt members of his Kachin flock facing the altar.   I slipped into a pew and watched the scene.*

The service was conducted in the Kachin (Jinghpaw) language.   I recognized most of those present.   Some were old and lined but among them were also a number of young men and women.   I wondered if, after the Padre had departed from their midst, as now seemed inevitable, they would forget their Christian teaching in a wild throw-back to their barbarous ancestors.   Would the Japs endeavor to introduce Shintoism and how would these kindly, lovable people react to it?

When the service was over I spoke to several of them.   They seemed to realize this service was likely to be the last for many a long day.   Yes, there were actually tears in the eyes of some of them. I could appreciate their feelings for the Rev. Crittle had carried on these Sunday services among the Kachin tribes people for more than fifteen years.   As I moved away in the direction of my bungalow, I too felt a lump in my throat.....

He described a disturbance in the town where law and order was breaking down.   *May 4th Early this morning Padre Crittle came over to discuss the situation and enquire about my plans, 'for' he said, 'I intend to leave for Mainghkwan without further delay.'   I told him I was overdue at Shaduzup where I had to inspect and pay for the work done by the Kachin villagers during April.   He could either wait my return to headquarters or we could go on together as far as Shaduzup.   Crittle said he would cycle out to a point in the jungle later in the afternoon, and wait for me there.*

Refugees were now passing by in enormous numbers but very few halted at Kamaing.   All seemed in a terrible hurry.   Many were fleeing to the Jade Mines and beyond but there were also many who were likely to make for the Hukawng Valley and disturb the peaceful little Kachin villages at Shaduzup and elsewhere.   The villagers would be terribly alarmed at the invasion of their jungle homes.

For the rest of the day I had not a spare moment.   The Chinese muleteers refused to accompany me saying they would return to Yunnan (China).   However, with the greatest difficulty I persuaded three of them to stand by with eleven mules.   The others packed up and went off, God knows where.

Lorries loaded with weary soldiers and civilians passed through to the west.   Dozens and dozens of carts carrying refugees and their children choked the road, while many hundreds of pedestrians trudged along with such belongings as they could manage to carry on their heads or as shoulder-loads.   About 4 p.m.   came the news that the food-store at Pahren Bum (mile 34) had been looted and that the godown staff with the exception of one Kachin Durwan had deserted.   I decided to go to the scene of the trouble by bus and let the mules come on later.

I walked out of my little wooden bungalow as I had walked out dozens of times before when going on tour and not troubling to give a second thought to the safety of my household effects.   This time I could not but feel anxious.   Authority hardly existed.   Hooligans had caused havoc in the town and their lust for destruction was by no means blunted....

...I reached a little camp of bamboo-and-thatch huts standing among trees at the edge of the jungle.   While the bus was unloading I hurried in the direction of the bamboo storehouses, about 100 yards distant. According to one rumour the buildings had been bombed by Jap planes and burnt down.   However the buildings were still there and intact.   I found the Kachin Durwan on duty but the other members of the staff had fled at the time of the looting.   'Something must be done' I thought, 'in an attempt to stop further pillaging.'   I despatched the Durwan to the headman of the adjacent Shan village.   When he appeared I gave him a written order to take charge of the foodstuffs still lying in the godown and issue them only to refugees.   There were crowds of people camping here for the night and the name 'Hukawng' was on all lips.   I was to learn that many thousands of people were taking this route in their flight to safety.....

Many refugees believed they were being closely followed by columns of Japanese soldiers, and others heard stories that the Japanese were advancing so fast on the Manipur Road that they were being shot at by their own planes.

CHAPTER EIGHT
May

'...I lay on my back all day. Carrying sections of tropical tree trunks had not agreed with it...' **Josephine**

Dr Russell described the moments when he too became one of the refugees: '...*At a time when every train was crammed to suffocation, every goods-wagon had dozens of people in it, with masses of kit, when men rode on top of the wagons, their possessions slung over the buffers, it was a problem how our party of about twenty-five men would manage to get into any train that might arrive. But our gracious God knew of our need, and provided for us. Left on the siding in the station yard was an empty first and second class coach which we were able to take over, and it was shunted on to the train that crawled into Mohnyin at 4pm on Monday afternoon, May 4th. By that time, though we knew it not, the Japanese had already occupied Bhamo, a short fifty miles away across the ranges, and were sweeping on to Myitkyina.*

Whilst the engine with its almost exhausted volunteer crew shunted us up and down the station marshalling the train, many friends from the village gathered round our coach to greet us for the last time. 'Back after the rains!' we called to them, but God alone knows when that day will be. At last the whistle blew, the engine hooted and our long train slowly began to draw out of Mohnyin. The familiar land-marks were behind us. The long trek to freedom had begun.

The train took them rapidly the forty miles to Sahmaw but then missed the station in the dark. .....*In the pitch darkness we climbed down at the side of the line, dragging our baggage from the coaches; whilst the rest of the party began to carry it back towards the station.*

There was a large sugar factory at Sahmaw....*Arrived at the Manager's bungalow, I found five or six of our friends,including two ladies, hard at work packing for a start next day on the road. The club building was turned over to us for the night, and a truck on their light railway on which to push our load of kit up from the station. It was not long before Gray, our trusty Army cook had fires burning on the lawn outside the club, rice cooking, and water for tea coming to the boil. This same Gray was to prove his worth many a time subsequently, conjuring appetizing meals apparently out of nothing, when stores were almost exhausted. But our meal, eaten from billy-cans at 1 a.m. of plain boiled rice and salt, was most welcome.*

Meanwhile Josephine was still trying to reach Katha on the boat. Not surprisingly she was worn out. '...*May 1st   I lay on my back all day. Carrying sections of tropical tree trunks had not agreed with it...*'

Many desperate people were becoming stranded and setting out on foot. In the evening of May 2nd the boat she was on reached Katha which was packed with refugees. The school party was still there, camping in a wooden house by the railway station. The bad news arrived that it appeared there were to be no more trains to Myitkyina. Katha was on a branch line, fourteen miles from Naba which was on the main railway line. Some people were walking to Naba hoping to get a train from there.

Josephine spent some time talking to the Evacuation authorities, but it seemed hopeless. '...*I and the older girls must walk out and the younger ones wait at Naba for a mainline train. If no train came, they would have to stay in neighbouring villages. The next problem was to find transport for the little ones to Naba, and if possible for the older ones to Indaw, fourteen miles to the south whence we should be in the trek westwards to the Chindwin...*'

Food was scarce and she and went to the DSP's house hoping for a meal and the loan of two cars. She found a dozen Europeans there all preparing to start the journey on foot the next day. Their hostility to her must have been hard to take: '...*The appearance of a young woman at this stage was decidedly a nuisance. They had taken the precaution of sending their own women folk away early, and here at the last minute was another. I understood what they felt, but disliked them for it all the same....they were kind and we had dinner, and I was promised two cars for the next day to ferry the small children to Naba and the older ones to Indaw. I went to bed.*'

It was a confusing situation. The next day a train had come in, but it was a hospital train taking patients from two boats that had just come up the river, and there was no room for civilians. Some children were taken by car to Naba and some to Indaw. Then there was an urgent message from the Evacuation officer. There was space after all on a packed train and the school party could be taken to Myitkyina. The children who had been taken to Naba could be picked up on the way.

The decisions made at this point had a huge impact on what happened next. It was decided that Josephine should stay and collect the two children from Indaw which was south of the railway line, and walk with them if they could not get to Myitkyina. Lillian Bald and John Derry went on the train with most of the children.

'...I was relieved to get them off. In Myitkyina, even if they had to wait for a plane for a day or two, they would be comparatively safe and not have to trek to India. I was uneasy about the possibility of air raids during the train journey. That afternoon they burnt all the paper money in the Treasury, and having dropped the silver in the middle of the river, they sank all the boats.'

She had dinner with the other group of Europeans. There were more complications. *'... Mr S who had taken the two older girls to Indaw that morning, told me that he had left them at Naba instead. People were being discouraged from trekking that way for it meant crossing the Chindwin too far south and the Japanese were advancing. It was probable then that the hospital train had picked up all four and I had only myself left to evacuate!*

The next morning, May 4th, Josephine was again very near to danger. They had an air raid in Katha. The railway was bombed and evacuees camping under the tree by the station were killed. The house where the children had been staying was burnt down. The European officials left that day, and the SDC took Josephine in his car to Naba where she could check that the four children had been picked up by the hospital train, and they had.

Josephine's plans were vague, and she still felt worried about the school party. The SDC was going to Indaw to start walking with his friends and she went in his car with him. She was dropped at a PWD bungalow at Indaw where a Major D gave her tea and said she must walk with his party.

In the circumstances, with air raids, very little food and water, the breakdown of law and order and almost no reliable trains running it was perhaps surprising that she felt she should try and follow the school party and Lillian and John to see if they had safely reached Myitkyina. Major D said a military train would be coming through, and he would ask for her to have a seat on it. She waited four hours but there was no train. *'...At 8 pm Major D came back. 'Come and have dinner,' he said. 'There will be no train after all. I should have to start walking to India tomorrow. There was a conference in the PWD bungalow. We had a meal on the grass outside and spreading out our bedding there, lay down to sleep. It was cool and the stars were bright.*

The Japanese were pushing forward to the Chindwin River in the west, northwards to Myitkyina, and up the route to the Burma Road in the east.

Not far from Katha, Dr Russell described visiting a deserted sugar factory at Sahmaw and being able to take some supplies ...*The great building usually humming with activity was silent, the mills and evaporating pans dimly seen in the light of the few electric bulbs still burning. All the labour had fled before this. ...Across one end of the factory was a solid wall many feet high of sacks of sugar, £70,000 worth, in a few hours perforce to be abandoned. The staff had tried to sabotage the mill engine, but lacking explosives there was little they could do. Even a fourteen-pound sledge hammer makes little impression on a sixteen-foot steel fly-wheel. It was the work of a few minutes to rip open the end of a sack and fill the two cushion covers we had brought with the best castor sugar...*

...However well some of our military friends may have slept, there was little space for some of us missionaries lying in a row on the floor of the veranda. The journey lay before us. After the first hundred miles, in the Hukawng valley very little was known about the country. We had no maps, no accurate information. It was reported that rice dumps had been prepared at certain places: some told us, 'on the best authority', that cars had been through as far as Ledo, in Assam: others said there there was no road at all! It seemed highly probable that we should have to carry all our kit on our own shoulders most of the way. Early that morning, Tuesday, May 5th, I turned to my Bible for comfort, and lit upon Psalm 61, the next in order for my reading, I read verse 6: 'I removed his shoulder from the burden.' 'That means transport', said I to myself. There followed verse 10: 'I am the Lord the God,....open thy mouth wide, and I will fill it'. And that means supplies!'

So it proved. Within a few hours our good friends of the sugar company had agreed to let us have the use of their Ford truck to carry all our baggage out to Kamaing, twenty-five shadeless, dusty miles away, whilst the party walked out light. Then they took us down to their big store godown, and virtually told us to help ourselves to provisions, torches, batteries, and other things of which we stood in need. Even in the twentieth century, the Lord does provide for His servants.

Back in January Josephine had shared a trench with George Tidey during an air raid in Rangoon. He was now with Dr Russell's party. '...*After the walking party had set out, the Rev. George Tidey of S.P.G, one of our Army chaplains and I who knew the road left with the lorry-load of kit for Kamaing. Two bicycles of those we had brought with us were left at Sahmaw, that we might use them to return to Kamaing in the evening, after we had brought back the lorry to its generous owners. Twelve miles out as we had arranged we stopped at the little half-way village to see if some sort of meal could be prepared for those who were following behind. There was a fairly large native house by the road, and to that we addressed ourselves. The owner appeared, all smiles, and reminded me that he had once attended our Mohnyin hospital, with profit to his health. He could not do enough for us, and immediately gave orders for a mighty curry to be prepared for the hungry warriors who would follow. Further, on our return journey in the evening, he had cups of tea and hard-boiled eggs ready for our refreshment.*

.....As we left Sahmaw, a sudden rainstorm swept down upon us from the hills. We sheltered in a stable, while the rain lashed down, and the track ran in rivers. Soon the sky began to clear, the storm rolled away and we resumed our journey. Raindrops flashed on the bushes, the air was cool and sweet. Before us, on the top of a rise, a single tall tree stood out against the sky. Far beyond it, lit by the westering sun, a mighty mass of tumbled hills lay like a blue backcloth to the scene. Behind us were our homes and possessions, and all the ordered life of many years. Before us, stretched the open road, and the Lord was good.

STORIES OF SURVIVAL IN BURMA

Details of the refugee route through the Hukawng valley
and over the Patkai mountains.

Copied from a handrawn map by Dr Russell.

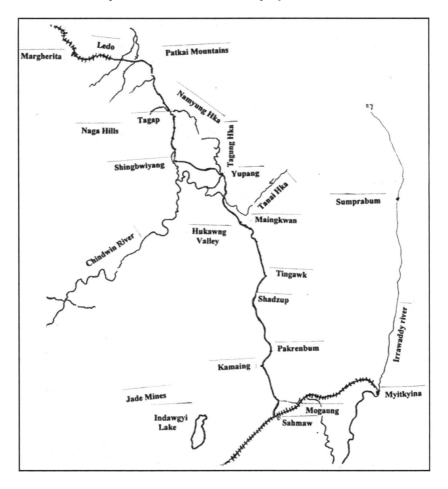

MAY

A chart written by Dr Russell

ESTIMATED DISTANCES FROM SAHMAW TO SHINGBWIYANG
["152 miles of motorable track"]

Sahmaw to Kamaing = 25 miles
Kamaing to Pakhrenbum = 9 miles
Pakhrenbum to Shaduzup to Tingawk = 43 miles
Tingawk to Walawbum to Mainghkwan = 28 miles
Mainghkwan to Tanai Hka (river) = 18
Tanai Hka to Yupang = 6 miles
Yupang to Shingbwiyang = 23 miles

DISTANCES FROM SHINGBWIYANG TO LEKHAPANI
["130 miles of mountainous jungle"]

Shingbwiyang to Chinglaw (3,000ft) = 7 miles
Chinglaw to Taga Hka = 8 miles
Taga Hka to Nathkaw (4,000ft) = 10 miles
Nathkaw to Tagap Ga (3,000ft) = 5 miles
Tagap Ga to Namyung Hka = 6.5 miles
Namyung Hka to Namlip = 15.5 miles
Namlip to Ngalang Ga (4,800ft) = 10 miles
Ngalang Ga to Tagung Hka = 8 miles
Tagung Hka to Nawngyang Hka = 9 miles
Nawngyang Hka (2000ft) to Shamlung = 6 miles

Shamlung – over **Pangsau Pass** (4,100ft) - to Nampong = 9.5 miles
Nampong (900ft) to Namgoi = 3 miles
Namgoi to Namchick = 8.5 miles
Namchick to Buffalo = 4 miles
Buffalo to Kumlao = 6 miles
Kumlao to N.Tirap = 6 miles
N.Tirap to Tipong = 4.5 miles
Tipong to Lekhapani (ITA refugee base) = 3 miles

Other distances from various road projects
In 1936 Govt cut "a four-foot mule track" from Tipong railhead to Namyung river = 90 miles. 1941 ITA built a "Jeep Road" from Lekhapani to Nampong (foot of Pangsau Pass) = 40 miles. In December 1942 work began on "Stilwell's Road" / "The Ledo Road". It was reckoned to be 103 miles from Ledo to Shingbwiyang.

The 152 miles of 'motorable' track became thick mud in the monsoon. Many mountains had to be climbed between Shingwiyang and Lekhapani.

CHAPTER NINE
May

'….The other two muleteers, addicted to opium, were invariably in a dazed state of mind…' **Captain Gribble**

Captain Gribble had travelled to Pakrenbum on a bus, followed by his mule train, and had been trying to restore order in a Kachin village where some Kachin workers had fled. *May 5th The mules had arrived about 9 p.m. the previous night escorted by a few of my Kachin followers…*

He described trouble with one muleteer, Lao Li, and *….The other two muleteers, addicted to opium, were invariably in a dazed state of mind. They had to smoke the drug every morning in order to rouse themselves sufficiently to tie up the packs. It was evident this morning that we would not be able to start marching before 8 a.m. whereas the stream of refugees invariably got under way at dawn.*

Despite being used to travelling in these country areas Gribble felt uneasy. *…After leaving our jungle camp the trees soon closed over the track, which remained slippery on the surface from the overnight storm. Our object was to camp in the jungle that night and reach Shaduzup the following morning before the air became too hot. I tried to convince myself that I was merely doing an irksome hot-weather tour but the crowd of refugees moving west and north was horribly disturbing….*

'…One thing was clear – the trek would be a terrible test of endurance before it was over. There was always another thought too – the Japs. Were they giving chase? Nobody knew and few now cared. They had but one thought, to hurry on through this jungle which as hour succeeded hour grew thicker and thicker and as day would succeed day likely to create a conviction in their minds that they had entered an area of eternal forest.

Looting was a big problem. On his way Gribble found a deserted thatched building where hundreds of bags or rice were stored. *…I knew a trustworthy Shan headman living at a village about two miles away and hurried over there to see him. He did not hesitate to take charge of the godown and assured me that if necessary he would use his villagers to back up his authority.*

Wilfred Crittle wrote about the lorries on the first stage of the journey:
Few were willing to take the lorries back for a second trip. They had a miscellaneous selection of human freight aboard. Some of them were filled entirely with British troops. Some came with Indian troops and others with a mixture of both. A number of them came loaded with

MAY

Chinese troops and a few had been taken over by Anglo-Indian or Indian civilians. All seemed possessed only with the idea of getting through as quickly as possible.

We put in a fairly hard day, helping, directing and advising. So many of the civilians on the road, English, Anglo-Indian alike were quite unused to the jungle – had in fact never been in it before – and were mortally afraid of it. Many too had heard of the ferocity of the Kachins and the headhunting activities of the Nagas. These travelled in fear of what might happen round the next corner. As conditions on the trek worsened and real hardships came along, these fears however all disappeared in the one activity of trying to sustain life until the end of the journey should be reached....

Dr Russell was on the road not far away. *There was no doubt that the cycles were seriously over-laden, but it was the best that could be done. In spite of all the efforts of Rushton our leader there were no coolies to be had, and there was no chance of an elephant to carry the stuff. The whole party realized the importance of pushing on from Kamaing with all speed that morning, for as the experienced ones kept on reminding us the Japs moved fast, and we could not regard ourselves as beyond their reach until we were in the hills, a hundred and thirty miles away.*

An additional reason for haste was the coming of the dreaded rains which would break towards the end of May, turning paths into streams and every marshy place into a veritable Slough of Despond.

Thus it followed that we loaded everything possible on to the eight cycles we had with us, and other loads on two ponies left for us in the Kamaing stable by the Rev W Crittle......and what was left of the stores and kit upon our own backs...

.....it was slow work pushing the loaded machines, but far better than abandoning the food stuffs that might mean all the difference between starvation and safety in later days.

Before us there lay more than a hundred miles of fairly level track much of it, in dry weather passable by motor transport (had we had any!) with at least two big rivers to cross before we left the Hukawng Valley and took to the hills. Then we should truly plunge into the unknown as far as any of our party were concerned. Down this road had come, in past years, the Kachin slaves who had escaped from their masters in the Valley, to settle in safety under the British rule round Kamaing.

There was much more traffic on the road that morning, all of it going in the same direction; to the West. The great exodus had begun, and thousands were pouring out from Mogaung, the nearest point on the railway away towards distant Assam. Big motor lorries whizzed by us as we trudged along in the dust, each one crowded with refugees. Full as they were, however, it was not long before members of our party, in ones and twos, had managed to beg lifts, throwing their loads in as well. In spite of a bad start, therefore, most of us were able to ride the nine miles to Pakrenbum, the next stage.

(sfr)

As two or three of us, the rearguard with the cycles, walked along the shadeless road, we came upon a scene common enough on the path of every retreat. The night before in the dark a heavily laden lorry had struck the side of a rough bridge, crashed down into the stream, and turned over. Three Indian women had been killed outright, several men

had sustained broken arms or collarbones, a child had been badly burnt. There lay the whole disconsolate party by the side of the road under a tree, their poor belonging scattered around them. We rendered what aid we could, but our medical supplies scanty enough in all conscience, had gone ahead. There was the chance that other lorries following would be able to pick them up and carry them on. There was nothing else to be done. We resumed our journey.

They reached the village recently described by Gribble. *At Pakrenbum by the side of the road had been erected a number of bamboo huts to house coolies working on the road. The coolies had gone, and in one of them we found shelter for the night. Not far from the camp site already swarming with our Indian fellow-travellers, three of us found a small stream, and were able to enjoy the first bath for three days, wallowing in the delicious cool water.*

......Others of us, with that spirit that is reputed to cause the lonely Englishman in the jungle to dress for dinner every night, resolved to wield the razor whenever opportunity offered, and it was seldom necessary to leave the rite for more than three days at a stretch. Do not judge us too harshly! It needs great resolution to advance the sickle to the standing corn, with rain dripping down one's back, wet socks and shoes on the feet, and the nearest water supply a mile away!....

...After our frugal supper, that evening, Captain Harris, one of our party returned in high spirits. He had secured a big lorry for our use on the morrow, with enough petrol to carry us to Maingkwan and beyond. It was with thankful hearts that we lay down to get what sleep we could on the hard bamboos. Once again, we had found that the Lord's hand was not shortened, nor His ear heavy.

The moment had arrived when Josephine needed to prepare for the walk. Unlike Dr Russell she had few supplies and had to carry her own possessions and rice rations from the beginning. She was following a different refugee trail which was used by the military but later became inaccessible. Significantly some rivers were still quite low at the height of the hot season before the monsoon. On May 5th after sleeping in the open she rose at dawn and sorted out what remained of her luggage, reducing it from 25 to 15 pounds, and leaving behind her Bible, prayer book and diary. She hoped her memory would be reliable.

She did however continue to write some sort of diary about the next few weeks. At the last minute Major D could not come, and she was sent on with three Burma businessmen from Rangoon. They were taken the first forty six miles by car to Pyinbone, and having slept in the heat of the day they walked fourteen miles by night and arrived at Mansi with the dawn. Later it appeared she was with a different walking group with a IFC captain who lent her some shoes and wrote a description of her in his diary.

On May 6th they walked all day, about fifteen miles. She wrote: '...*I ..was determined that the party should not be held up because there was a woman in it.*' She threw away her blanket and was told she would need it later in the hills. They passed the body of a soldier face downwards in the grass with his kit around him, and slept in the jungle near a village called Magyigone. She did not know that this was the day when the school party at Myitkyina airfield were to be caught in terrible air raids.

On May 7th they found the Evacuation officer and about forty of his staff at Kyauksegyi. They were camping on a good site near the U-Yu river. She was glad to find some women to talk to, and to rest for two nights while some rafts were built for them to travel along the river. Someone gave her another blanket and quinine tablets with strict orders to take them every day as she had no mosquito net.

CHAPTER TEN
May

'...refugees.....trailing along in ant-like lines – tall men, short men, women, children, babies in arms, men with wounds, old men hobbling along with the pathetic illusion that they would soon come to a place where they could rest and find enough food to stave off hunger and exhaustion...' **Captain Gribble**

Captain Gribble was making progress on his pony with his eleven mules. *May 6ᵗʰ   We reached Shaduzup about 11 a.m.   All morning the sky was full of aeroplanes as they passed to and fro from a northern aerodrome in Burma, but I had only just reached the camp when I heard the crump, crump and crump of bombs falling in the direction of Myitkyina.   That place, as the crow flies, was not very distant from Shaduzup. "That will be the end of the evacuation by air," I thought, and so it proved for no aeroplanes were seen during the afternoon or on subsequent days.* Later Josephine was to hear news about Lillian and John and the school party.

With his local knowledge of places and people and his work with the Burma Frontier Service Gribble's journey was in many ways different from others around him. He was often looked after and fed by local village chiefs where news was exchanged and advice given on both sides. He was concerned that the lives of the Kachin and Naga people were being turned upside down by the thousands of refugees tramping through their villages and using their houses for shelter. Later he was overwhelmed with worries about his own survival, but even at that final stage he had contact with local guides.

My camp site and rest-house were crowded with refugees but the Kachins, who were expecting me, had erected my tent in a plantation near a Kachin house. I felt pleased about this thoughtful arrangement for there was a lot of work to be done and I needed elbow room. I visited troops of refugees moving through the village along the route to the Hukawng, trailing along in ant-like lines – tall men, short men, women, children, babies in arms, men with wounds, old men hobbling along with the pathetic illusion that they would soon come to a place where they could rest and find enough food to stave off hunger and exhaustion. Petty thefts of every kind occurred but in order to pacify the villagers I told them I would be responsible for loss of livestock. They enquired whether their women and children would be safe but I could not guarantee that and I advised their removal to the field huts in their

their plantations. May 7th   This morning I received a note from the Evacuation Officer who had passed by overnight in a Jeep, requesting me to go on to the Hukawng and meet him at a place called Taihpa. Here was a pretty fix indeed for I had only brought a limited quantity of rations and there were already many calls on what I possessed.   How long would the food last?   It was tragic to think of an evacuation of refugees through the famine stricken Hukawng
....I spent most of the day with the Kachin villagers.   I paid them their wages, answered many questions, and received many assurances of loyalty...

Wilfred Crittle wrote: *The armed police did not wish to come any further as they were afraid to be away from their wives and families any longer.   So Gribble paid them all off, giving them, beside a present of money a rifle or a shotgun each, together with as many rounds of ammunition as could be spared.   They got out of their uniforms and became ordinary Kachins for the return journey.*

Captain Gribble experienced more hospitality in the local village.   *In the evening the carcass of a deer was brought along.   It was soon skinned. A fire flared up and choice morsels were placed.   In half an hour the feast was ready.   The villagers gathered round and made merry.   It was an incredibly cheerful party and ended with stories of the days when the Du Ni (English) first appeared among the Kachins, and of the battles that ensued.   The trouble in Burma was incredible, unbelievable to these friendly, likeable people who were certain that the Du Ni would be victorious before many moons had passed.*
May 8th Runners arrived during the night to say that Mainghkwan had been looted and that the whole population had fled to the jungle. Mainghkwan was the only area of importance in the Hukawng where rice was grown in quantity.   Awful thought.   "The Shans no doubt will have gone to their relations in the Daru Valley," I surmised, "but what will the Kachin villagers living in the Hukawng do for food?"...I must hurry on....There was only one way – by aircraft.   Somehow or other help would come.
    Gribble tried to make progress towards Mainghkwan, overstretching the strength of the mules and frustrated by his drugged muleteers.   *...I began to loathe the sight of them. They were too calm, too oblivious of what was going on around them.   However they were merely jungle people from Yunnan and led a very hard life. Perhaps, in their own way*

they knew better than we did what was in store for all of us.
...That night when our little meal was over and the heat and fatigue of the
day were less heavy on our minds, we allowed ourselves to indulge in a
few reflections covering the past few months. The battlefront had
collapsed and what a shock it was. What a mess! Reproaches,
recrimination, all seemed futile. Was racial tiredness and decay
anything to do with this debacle? We tried to discern something of the
shape of things to come but gave it up.

Loneliness and sadness led him to desperate thoughts: *...I fell asleep*
with some soothing, comforting words running through my mind: "I have
seen much to hate here – much to forgive. But in a world where
England is finished and dead, I do not wish to live".

At this time Dr Russell's wife Muriel's was arriving in India and he was
later to learn of her experiences: . *...Some seventy minutes after leaving*
Myitkyina the great aircraft, her engines merely ticking over, circled
over the emergency landing ground of Dinjan in Assam. In obedience to
the order all the passengers laid hold of the long rail running above their
heads, ready for the landing. Smoothly she swooped down; a slight
bump, a bounce or two and she was safely on the ground. As the weary
travellers descended from the plane a friendly English tea-planter in a
homely green pork-pie hat stood ready to receive them....
The town of Dibrugarh is some twenty miles from the airfield. It
stands upon the south bank of the great river Brahmaputra, here some
four miles wide in flood time. Bumping along the dusty road, Muriel
seated on the floor on a spare tyre, the children held by the other
missionary ladies, to them the journey seemed long indeed and
tedious.....two hundred miles in three hours from Burma to Assam,
across a well-nigh trackless waste of mountains and jungle is good
travelling for the east. It was hardly three o'clock on that eventful
Sunday afternoon.

A telegram about their safe arrival was sent to the Deputy
Commissioner at Myitkyina. *...needless to say it was never delivered, for*
on that very day Japanese planes heavily bombed the Myitkyina
aerodrome. I was already seventy-five miles from Mohnyin on the first
stage of the long and dangerous trek to Assam and eventual safety.

Muriel and her children stayed in an evacuation camp in Dibrugarh
Roman Catholic Cathedral. Again attempts were made to send news, not
knowing how chaotic communications were becoming *...Before they*
slept Muriel wrote a letter to me, away over the mountains in Burma.

One of the helpers said he would be flying back to Myitkyina in a day or two and promised to post it there. The letter was duly despatched but neither it nor any other word reached me anxiously waiting across the frontier....

It was May 9th and Josephine had been resting for two days at the camp at Kyauksegyi near the U-Yu river. There was trouble getting rafts built, and when they were built there was the prospect of slow progress along the river. Those who wanted to set off left at four that afternoon. This group had a few Indian servants to carry luggage and a horse to carry the rice.

It was a remote area. It is likely someone in the group knew where they were going. The track through hilly and thickly wooded jungle was very difficult and impossible in places for the horse, so they waded through the river. It was not too deep and the bed was sandy. They walked barefoot in the river all Sunday and half of Monday. It was tiring but cool and they slept in the open at night. One of the Indians was bitten by a snake, and an Indian doctor made an incision around the bite which only developed into a swelling for a few days.

Dr Russell's group had rested at the village of Pakrenbum, with news of a lorry they could use the following day. ...*Twenty-four hours later, thanks to our newly-acquired transport we lay under the stars at Tingawk, forty-three miles further on our way. There had been time for a meal at the Kachin village of Shaduzup, beautifully situated above its fast-flowing river, and a bath in the clear water. The last few miles of the journey in the fading daylight, had proved the most eventful of the day. A long stretch of the track, hemmed in by the big trees of the virgin jungle, had been soaked by a thunderstorm, and then churned into mud by the passing traffic. In spite of all the skill of Captain Bailey our expert driver, our lorry skidded, slowed and stuck fast. The spinning wheels cut deep trenches for themselves. We dragged branches and wood from the jungle, thrusting them into the mud beneath the wheels, We lightened the lorry, we pulled and pushed. It was all in vain. Was our lorry to be abandoned already, like others we had passed on the road? When the position seemed hopeless, there came shouldering through the jungle an elephant, one of those belonging to a timber firm, with its dragging chain trailing behind. For a handsome tip, the mahout* (elephant driver) *hitched his great beast to the front of our lorry. Whilst the engine roared, the elephant trumpeted, and we cheered; the lorry stirred, moved, and was dragged through the hundred yards of slough on to the firm road again. We climbed in and reached the camp as darkness fell.*

A photo Dr Russell took of his party with their lorry in early May

It was the day after Captain Gribble had felt deep despair. *May 9th   All day long we saw groups of refugees; some of them halted by the way side. Many looked as if they expected to be entombed for ever in the bowels of that dark forest land.   Some said they had already travelled hundreds of miles after abandoning their homes in the Shan States.   Many had escaped from Mandalay and places below that city.   Some were settlers from northern districts in Burma. It was an astonishing situation, a tragedy unique in history.   What terror had driven these peace-loving people to seek refuge in such a wilderness? Even grass had become scarce along the track.   Scanty patches of grass had been eaten clean and transport animals, already showing signs of exhaustion, were far from their journey's end.*

We reached Maingkwan late in the afternoon, and as the sun slowly sank behind the uninhabited hills to the west its weak rays shone on a deserted village.   Mainghkwan was deserted.   The inhabitants had fled in terror to jungle places at the first sign of panic-stricken refugees trailing hurriedly through the village....We proceeded to a spot just north of the village and found shelter for the night.

Dr Russell had a brief lift in a jeep driven by 'an official' while others were in the lorry which had further struggles on the bad road. They too were about to reach Maingkwan. *...Later in the morning we stopped to pick up a little Gurkha family trudging wearily on their way. The small boy of the party, perched precariously on top of the kit in the back, was one large grin as we rattled on our way. The mother, burdened with an infant, sighed thankfully as she saw the long miles drop behind. Did they ever reach the land of safety, still so far ahead? We shall never know.*

His group arrived at a village, and preoccupied with their own problems they seem unaware that the local villagers felt threatened and had fled. *The jeep dropped me outside our little hospital at Maingkwan soon after midday. There I was able to exchange a few words with the Rev.C.E. Darlington, whose wife and two-months old baby had left that morning, with a party of women. To carry some of the party they had Maggie, the elephant belonging to the Mission, of which more later. An hour or two after Darlington had gone on after his wife, the lorry brought my friends to the door, to my surprise and relief. So bad was the road, over which I had travelled in the jeep, that I felt sure they would not be able to reach Mainghkwan that day. But I had reckoned without the skill of our drivers.*

When the possibility of an ultimate evacuation through the Hukawng Valley, of which Maingkwan is the centre had first been suggested, the far-sighted Field Secretary of the Mission had formed a small dump of useful stores in the bungalow. On these stores we were able to draw, and the most valuable did they prove. Those of our number who had no blanket were supplied from the hospital. But it was not all gain. As it seemed highly probable that a few miles farther on we should be without any transport, we went through our packs again, weeding out everything not absolutely essential for the march. As it turned out, though we were not to know it, our fears were groundless. Save for two days, we had some transport throughout our journey.

Before we left Maingkwan, that Saturday afternoon, May 9th, we heard the distant hum of a plane. As it drew nearer, we scattered under the surrounding trees; it might prove to be a Jap. Soon two big aircraft came into view, and circled over the village. The experts in our company pronounced them British, and it was not long before the friendly intentions of our visitors were made manifest. As they swept low over the house, one after another dark objects fell from the planes, parachutes opened, gleaming white in the sun, and swayed to the ground. Several of our people hurried off into the jungle where they had fallen, and

*returned with packets of biscuits, tins of bully beef, and a paper giving
information about the efforts being made in Assam to send relief down
the road. It was our first contact with the life-saving labours of the
R.A.F How we longed by some means to climb up into the big planes
that roared overhead! They were only an hour's journey from safety, we
had three weeks to go!*

R.A.F. planes overhead   (sfr)

*It was not until late afternoon that we finally moved away on the next
stage of our travels, but the night's rest had done us all good. Our stores
were replenished, our bodies refreshed, and our spirits encouraged by
the knowledge that the Burma refugees were not forgotten. Further, a
jeep had been abandoned over for our use, and it was to prove of great
value.*

*The next eighteen miles took us six hours of hard travelling! We broke
no world's record for speed, but we can truthfully say there was not a dull
moment! But for the jeep we should have been beaten by the mud, again
and again. As it was, there were at least half a dozen big lorries left
abandoned, hopelessly stuck in the appalling sloughs, past which we*

had to edge our way, slowly and painfully. Rickety wooden bridges swayed under the weight of the lorry, even though the driver wisely insisted on our unloading it before he made the attempt. Had a bridge collapsed, the road would have been blocked for all those coming behind; it was a solemn thought.

'Our lorry crawls cautiously over a flimsy bridge May 9th' (sfr)

Darkness overtook us, and we still had many miles to go. The jeep's headlights lit up the track, and the lorry followed close behind, the feeble ray of a torch held by the jeep's passengers showing up some of the snags. In spite of an hour's work by two expert mechanics earlier in the day on the lighting set of the lorry, the fault had not been detected, and the lights would not work. Then, when we were stuck for a time in deep mud, there happened what seemed to us little short of a miracle. Saying: "It's no good! You see, they won't work!" Captain Bailey, our driver snapped the switch again in desperation. Instantly the big headlights blazed out, and shone brilliantly until we reached our journey's end! Some of us, perhaps all saw in the incident the finger of God.

To the two of us who rode on the back of the jeep, the sight of the two brilliant circles of light following carefully behind caused moments of acute anxiety. At one point, where the track was only just wide enough for the big lorry to pass, a massive tree trunk still further encroached on the path, as it went round the corner. We saw the lights tilting, tilting. Surely the lorry was over! No! While we held our breath, it slowly came back on to an even keel, and the danger was past.

There was one bad patch, a real driver's nightmare. At each side of a deep mud-filled hollow and at the bottom were derelict lorries axle-deep. A tree-trunk lay across the path. Careful measurement proved that even if the mud did not stop our lorry the available space was several inches too narrow to let it pass. All our efforts failed to move the middle derelict more than an inch or two. Its engine was dead, and could not help. But one of our party had been a bus-driver. He climbed into the driving-seat, put it into reverse and, whilst we all pushed, drove it a foot or two back with the self starter. The way was clear. The jeep's dragging-chains were attached, the engines roared, the mud flew, we pushed, and our precious vehicle slowly drew out of that dreadful place.

Midnight found the company supping off bully-beef and tea, under the light of the lorry, on the sandy banks of the Tanai Hka, a wide river, the upper reaches of the Chindwin. A big bamboo raft, slung from a cane rope, ferried carts and people over in daylight, but crossing was out of the question until morning. We lay down in rows on the sloping sand banks and hoped for sleep. But the constant flicker of lightning and the distant growl of thunder was ominous.

In the small hours the storm burst upon us. Hastily rolling up bedding we took refuge wherever we could, in or under the lorries standing round. There together with many Indians we sat huddled and waited for the dawn.

CHAPTER ELEVEN
May

'The village, like so many towns and villages in Burma was reduced to ashes….' **Captain Gribble**

Captain Gribble also described a storm: *May 10th .... About midnight it became oppressively hot and still. All the forest seemed to be holding its breath, as though about to do something dreadful. The suspense of waiting was broken suddenly by thunder, rain and wind, all rising in violence until, at about an hour before dawn, they reached a pitch such as I had not believed possible. Then while the forest was crashing with falling boughs and trees, the heart suddenly went out of the storm and it was over. Still the refugees went hurriedly on, as if the devil was after them; and the ground, which had been soaked by the rain, looked and trod like a ploughed field...*

May 11th. The sun shone again and the warmth of it made us feel more cheerful. The monsoon was still holding off. We sat down to our breakfast of tea, porridge, and a 'chapatti' made of flour. Suddenly the Shan Akyiwa appeared trembling with excitement. He said. "I took my family away to the jungle and have just returned to wait for you. Now the village is on fire." I leapt to my feet. Sure enough I saw wisps of smoke trailing to the sky and by the time I arrived at the village it was one great plain of fire. Not a soul was to be seen.

For fifty seven years the Akyiwa had lived in Mainghkwan, watched it grow, taken the greatest share in its welfare, and seen it prosper. He said, "People entered the village during the night and ransacked it. This morning they set fire to the houses and decamped along the track going in a northerly direction."

I tried to console the Akyiwa and told him he was lucky to have got his family and the other inhabitants to a place of safety. But, like him, I felt horribly miserable at all this devastation, this upheaval among friendly, timid jungle folk who had very little inkling that fate would treat them so harshly, so crushingly, and without warning. The village, like so many towns and villages in Burma was reduced to ashes.

Nkum La, who had accompanied me on many visits to the Hukawng told me today that he was anxious about his family and wanted to go back and look after them. I was sorry to part with him.....That night we discarded all surplus kit and belongings, retaining only a spare shirt and blankets. Our few mules were required to carry our rapidly dwindling store of food. A young officer of a British regiment joined us. He said he had orders to proceed to India and report to the nearest military base!

He was armed with a rifle and pistol but was without food. At this stage, rifles were useful for shooting fish in the river, but that was all. Even the birds had caught the panic and taken flight. During the whole trek I do not remember seeing half a dozen winged creatures, other than vultures!

Dr Russell's group had had a disturbed night, sheltering where they could from the violent storm. *The slow light of morning revealed a sullen river hissing under the rain which beat down from a leaden sky. Across the ferry could be seen a steep slope, churned into deep and slippery mud: half-way up it a cart was stuck. the shouts of the men who were vainly trying to push it to the top of the bank came faintly to us across the water. Five or six other carts stood at the river's edge on our side, waiting their turn on the ferry. Higher up the bank was a line of abandoned lorries.*

Tired and wet, our spirits sank low. It seemed a hopeless dawn. It is under such circumstances that one realizes afresh the value of prayer, the tremendous strength to be found in the promises of God. However overwhelming appeared the difficulties of the way, His grace was sufficient, His strength was made perfect in human weakness.

A few hours before our arrival, so we learnt, someone had tried to get his jeep on to the raft and over the river. The heavy car had tipped the raft up, run off into deep water and had been lost; the bamboo craft too had been damaged, thereby imperilling the safety of those yet to cross. To some of us it seemed wiser to abandon all hope of getting our jeep over, and to reconcile ourselves to shouldering our heavy burdens. In any case, it was pointed out, only six miles beyond the Tanai Hka was an even greater river, the Tarung Hka, and no vehicle could be ferried across that.

But our drivers were as skilful as they were enthusiastic. Collecting odd pieces of wood and all the leather cushions from the driving seats of the derelict lorries, they built a ramp up which the jeep was driven on to the raft. The water rose above the bamboo deck, but it still floated and on an even keel. Cautiously the craft was pulled along the cane rope by several pairs of lusty arms, until the further bank was reached. The ramp was re-built. Captain Millom started his engine, engaged the clutch and drove straight off the raft, and up the treacherous slope without a check. The jeep was over!

STORIES OF SURVIVAL IN BURMA

Crossing the river with the jeep on the raft   (sfr)

By this time the sky had cleared, and a watery sun was shining.   Spirits rose.   The baggage was ferried across, and the heaviest items, a sack of sugar, and another of flour and other valuable stores were loaded into our trusty jeep.   Even then every man was loaded with sundry packs, but it was with lighter hearts that we set off down the jungle path, trying to pick the firmest track through the deep mud.

For three miles all went well.   Then came disaster.   A dip in the road held a pool of liquid mud, two feet deep and more. The jeep skidded from the firmer side right into the slough and stuck fast.   Even the front-wheel drive could find nothing on which to grip.

Struggling with the jeep on Sunday May 10th   (sfr)

The intrepid members of our party, braving the mud, tried to push, but

there was hardly any foothold. The loads were taken out. As the sack of sugar came over the side, it slipped, and gently but quite firmly it pressed friend Pearson deep into the warm mud. Whatever may have been the feelings of the victim, to the onlookers it was the cause of much rude and noisy mirth. Fortunately a near-by stream afforded facilities for the removal of the newly-acquired top-dressing.

Another jeep, happening along, added the powerful persuasion of its towing chains to our efforts, but it was all in vain. Ours was well and truly stuck, and there it remained. We bade it a sad farewell.

Now surely the time had arrived for us to shoulder our packs? But no! Our need was met even as it arose. Round the corner came a long line of empty bullock carts returning home from the ferry in front. All the arts of blandishment at my command, couched in my best Burmese were successful in persuading the leader of the convoy to turn three of his vehicles round, and for a consideration to carry our baggage the remaining three miles to our destination for the night.

Picture us then that Sunday evening, safely lodged in a tumbledown Jinghpaw hut high on the bank of the wide Tarung Hka River. Over the fire the acrid smoke which found its way more quickly into our watering eyes than through the holes in the roof, boiled a mighty dish of stew. A tin full of tea comforted our hearts. Our bedding was spread on the sounder parts of the rickety floor. The day's exertions were behind us.

Before we lay down to rest, by the flickering light of a few small candles, we gathered round the Word of God. In that remote and ruined hut, far from home, the majestic words of Psalm 91 brought comfort and strength. Voices were raised in the solemn music of the world's best known hymn: 'Abide with me, fast falls the eventide'. After a short word of exhortation, heads were bowed in prayer, and the party was once again commended into the gracious keeping of Him to Whom the darkness and the light are both alike. Our evening worship ended, we lay down to sleep.

On May 11th Josephine also described a storm. After much walking in the shallow river they cut across fifteen miles of hilly country, and joined it again at Mainkaing. They had a violent storm as they slept in the open. '... *So putting on our raincoats, we sat on our bundles to keep them dry. At 3.30 a.m. the servants lit a large fire. How they could do it with such speed when everything is drenched after rain, I shall never understand. We dried and warmed ourselves and drank plain tea.*

STORIES OF SURVIVAL IN BURMA

Dr Russell's account of events on May 11th continued with much detail. *The Tarung Hka was without doubt a formidable proposition. Little short of a quarter of a mile in width and very swift, even in the dry weather; a few days rain would render it impassable by any. It was desirable to put it behind us without delay. From the top of the steep bank, on which we stood, a rough path led down to a stony beach. Across the river whipping back and forth in the strong current stretched a cane rope, supported in midstream by long poles driven into the bed. Along the rope crept from side to side the two bamboo rafts which represented the means of escape of the thousands on the Assam road. On the further bank, beyond a wide reach of stones, lay the scattered huts of the village of Yupang. Far to the North, in grim isolation rose a line of frowning black hills, their crests worn into fantastic shapes.*

Waiting patiently to cross the Tarung Hka Monday May 11th (sfr)

Awaiting their turn to cross were hundreds of Indians of many races, our fellow-travellers. A line of bullock-carts stretched up the track. As each raft reached the bank, a swarm of would-be passengers rushed at it, and

and in a few minutes crowded it far beyond its capacity, so that the water rose across the deck. There ensued a pretty bedlam ,latecomers being pushed off, others waist-deep in the water, trying to climb on unobserved, every man shouting at the top of his voice all the time. It was not until Padre Rushton and some others of our party constituted themselves controllers of the traffic, that progress was made. Then, for the whole of that Monday morning, May 11th , with voices and sticks they kept back the frantic crowds, allowing on board only what the raft would safely bear.

The crowds on the rafts and the river bank   (sfr)

It was not until the afternoon that our party crossed. As we were waiting our turn a party of Indian solders rode down the bank, and with show of arms commandeered the rafts for themselves and their kit before

the eyes of the hundreds who had waited so long.   Remonstrance was in vain, force held the trump card for a time.   It is pleasing to record that when this group reached Assam, retribution overtook it at the hand of the authorities for its behaviour upon the road.

*   As we gathered upon the further bank that evening, a fine sight met our eyes.   A big party belonging to one of the timber firms working in Burma was coming up behind us, and a long line of their elephants was being driven into the water for the crossing.   Some thirty beasts reached a sand-bank rising out of the river, but the main stream lay beyond.   A great tusker led the way, and swam strongly through the rushing current. Some bolder ones followed, but many smaller and less courageous, turned back   Only about half the number reached our side, the rest strode into the further jungles and were seen no more. As we ate our evening meal, the news from far-away England came to us from a wireless set brought by one of the elephants.   A reference to the state of affairs in Burma caused us sardonic amusement.*

Wilfred Crittle wrote of a conflict in which Gribble intervened. A misunderstanding had arisen during the night between a young Chinese soldier and the Kachins whose hut he was using. *...Green doubled round the house and arrived at the spot in time to see a Chinese soldier preparing to shoot a Kachin villager...'...It was not until Green put the muzzle of his pistol in our Chinese friend's ear that he lowered his rifle and behaved like a rational human being once more.   Fortunately General Lim was still in the village and so Gribble was able to get him to settle matters and explain to the soldier that robbery of his rifle had not been intended....Later that evening Gribble got General Lim and the senior Sikh officer together and it was arranged that on the morrow Chinese and Sikhs should provide an armed guard for the ferry so that all people should be taken across in order of their arrival regardless of race and sex.   This sounded very nice but when we rose next morning we found that the General and his satellites had crossed by canoe and the Sikhs had commandeered a raft and disappeared so there was still the same chaos as before...'*

CHAPTER TWELVE
May

'…We should not get to Homalin in a week at this rate. And meanwhile, where were the Japanese? We had been warned that we should cross the Chindwin by the 15th…' **Josephine**

On May 12th Josephine 's group had reached a small river and had breakfast in a remote PWD bungalow. They bathed in the river and washed and dried some clothes in the midday sun. They were able to get a raft and set out at 4 pm. '…. *Such enjoyable anticipation: a day or two gliding lazily down the U-Yu river to the Chindwin…after a few minutes we stuck on a sandbank, and we all got off to push the raft clear. We spent the rest of the day going about half a mile having to cope with sandbanks all the time. We tied up at dusk by a sandy clearing, ate the last tin of beef with our rice and went to bed. There was another storm that night - and another fire in the early hours to get dry and warm.*
May 13th The raft was cut into three with the hope that each section, being lighter, would avoid the sandbanks. But it was not much better and we travelled about only five miles. We should not get to Homalin in a week at this rate. And meanwhile, where were the Japanese? We had been warned that we should cross the Chindwin by the 15th.'

At this stage Captain Gribble seemed to be behind Dr Russell's party. On May 12th he wrote that after a hard day's marching they reached the Tanai Hka. He noticed a village downstream on the other side: '…*our immediate interest was forced by the arrival of a number of Kachins who had apparently crossed the river by raft-ferry. The Taihpa Duwa, a stout, bearded little man, had come over with the ferrymen to help us across the river and to give me the news. "For ten days," he said, "refugees have been passing through my village in a continual stream, following the trail to Shingbwiyang.." "Stay at my house," he added, "you will be away from the filth of the jungle." As all of us were feeling exhausted I was only too glad to find shelter in a Kachin house….I remember walking to the Akyiwa's house about 11 p.m. amidst the smoke, chatter and coughing of refugees, some camping in the open, some under and in the houses in the village. The great warmth of the Akyiwa's house made me drowsy and I remembered nothing else until the next morning.*
May 13th For several hours this morning the rain fell in a steady stream and I looked at the sky with anxiety. I feel that the storm at Mainghkwan was a warning that the monsoon weather was about to engulf us. What would happen when the rivers became torrents? The

STORIES OF SURVIVAL IN BURMA

Tarung River, eight miles north of Taigpa, was the devil of a river in the rainy season. Already the water had risen several feet and it seemed to me it was not without reason that the Kachins called it the 'waters of death'!

...Among the crowds of refugees resting or hurrying by were Europeans, Indians, in some instances accompanied by Burmese wives and children; Gurkhas, Anglo Burmans; many varieties of women and babies in arms. I answered hundreds of questions. "The R.A.F. is dropping food supplies at a place called Shingbwiyang," I said, "there is a camp there and you should hurry on. The rains are near."

At this point Gribble mentions Dr Russell. He must have met up with this other party. *...We distributed some quinine and Russell bandaged a few leg wounds. I noticed a few Chinese soldiers and among them several stretcher cases. As I saw the stretcher-bearers marching with their burdens I was filled with admiration at their devotion. I saw many carts and transport bullocks, but I knew they would have to be abandoned in a day or two for the track now entered broken ground with numberous ravines to negotiate and rain was rapidly turning the track into a muddy squashy mess.*

Dr Russell. *...The following morning a fresh problem awaited us. An official known to some of us reached the river with a string of a dozen pack mules and three ponies. We had hopes that he might be willing to lend or sell us a few of his beasts so badly needed to transport of vital stores. In any case, without our help, he would have great difficulty in getting the animals across the river. We resolved to give him our aid.*

There followed a gallant piece of work by Padres Rushton and Tidey, and Lieut. Bruce. The three swam to the sand-bank in the river which was separated by a shallow channel from the bank on which the animals were waiting. These were then driven into the water and so across to the sandbank. With considerable difficulty they were collected together and persuaded to enter the main channel. Again and again, faced with the swift current, the obstinate beasts turned back, and started to graze on the course vegetation springing from the sand. At last, the swimmers, chilled as they were with the long delay, succeeded in getting the leading pony to adventure the crossing; driven with shouts and stones the others followed, and all safely reached the bank, where we awaited them.

The owner of the animals was no doubt grateful for our help, but our

MAY

hopes were unfulfilled and he did not see his way to assisting us. That afternoon our party started off once again, but this time each man was heavily burdened. The twenty-three gruelling miles that lay before them took until late the following evening and it was a desperately weary party that straggled into Shingbwiyang, long after dark, on Wednesday May 13.

I had stayed behind at the ferry, with a man suffering from an attack of high fever, a member of the party of our friend the official. As a result most of my baggage was carried by his pack mules the next day and we were able to walk to whole twenty-three miles in one day, thus rejoining my friends in front. The road was fairly level, but the mud, deep and tenacious made the going very heavy. As we ploughed along it was astonishing to see the stocky little members of a Chinese ambulance party carrying on stretchers shoulder high their wounded comrades. Their persistence and endurance is all the more remarkable and praiseworthy when one realizes that some of those same wounded were carried in that fashion more than two hundred miles across plains and over mountains. Truly their spirit is unconquerable.

At last in the gathering dark, the jungle opened out. The lights of many fires, the hum of voices, the unclean odours of a camp-site told us that our long day was over. We entered Shingbwiyang, tiny Jingpaw village, one hundred and fifty miles from the railway, and the end of the Hukawng Valley.

Wilfred Crittle wrote: '*...we heard on a radio jettisoned by one of the forestry men, the broadcast of Sir Reginald Dormal-Smith, the Governor of Burma. Speaking from Delhi he told the world just how well everything had been organized and how magnificently everyone had stuck to their posts. We who were in the middle of the chaos were "not amused" and loud were the jeers with which his speech was greeted: officers and civilians alike united in making caustic comments on British propaganda....*'

CHAPTER THIRTEEN
May

' ...His task it was to feed the starving, to control the lawless and to bury the dead....' **Dr Russell**

A day before, on May 12th a group of young soldiers had arrived at Shingbwiyang, and in this group was Sergeant Benjamin Katz who later wrote his remarkable story. Already working there was Neil North, a young political officer who together with Katz bravely stayed on in the remote village until September. Dr Russell described his meeting with North.

On one side of a small paddy-field, between it and a sluggish stream stood three Jingpaw huts. Across the field had been built several go-downs, intended as rice-dumps to feed the coolies who were to have come as road-builders. Every available foot of space in huts, under and around them, was occupied by refugees. Nearly all were Indians of various races, Punjabis, Tamils, Ooriyas. There were some Anglo-Indians, and two or three parties of Europeans. To control these hundreds and to issue daily supplies of rice and what other stores were available was one young political officer, Neil North, an old friend of ours, who had gallantly stuck to his post. His task it was to feed the starving, to control the lawless and to bury the dead. To the missionaries of our party and to me in particular he showed great kindness and hospitality. It was a rare treat to sit down to a table again and to eat from a china plate.

Two nights we spent in the little village, resting before the arduous travelling that lay in front of us. The hills rose like a wall beyond the river, and our way lay over them. Two or three times each day the big planes from India swept over the open paddy-field, dropping the supplies that alone kept the crowds from starvation.

First came several parachutes bearing cases of Army biscuits or tinned milk. Then on each run up the small space the figures we could clearly see at the open door of the aircraft would cast down sacks full of tea, rice or sugar, with tins of bully beef or milk inside. Like sticks of bombs they came crashing to the earth, people scattering in all directions from beneath them. Some fell in the jungle beyond the village and were lost in spite of search. One smashed through the roof of a hut, another raised a mighty splash in a pool. Then, its work of mercy ended, the plane would sweep round, its crew waving to us below and away over the hills.

When once the supplies were on the ground prompt action was necessary to forestall looting. Our officers and men played their part in this, superintending the collection of all bags and cases, and then helping to form and control the long queues of hungry people.

Hunger was not the only foe that attacked the camp. The dreaded cholera took its toll. In a dark corner of a hut, or huddled under a go-down one found its victims, cold and racked with cramps. Even the simplest drugs were scarce; many a life was lost, that might have been saved by timely treatment.

During our stay in this unhappy village we tried once again to obtain mules, but in vain. The night before we left however something far better was provided for our need.

Maggie   (sfr)

Crittle and Rushton announced in triumph that the Mission elephant

had been handed over to our party, and that the Jingpaw mahout had agreed, albeit reluctantly, to come with us for the next four days. 'Reluctantly' is the right word! It had taken two hours of intensive persuasion and the promise of Rs 200/- to the young fellow to incline him to agree. The offer of a sporting gun belonging to one of our party was the final bribe and that made up his mind for him. When lives are at stake money loses its importance!

On May 14th Captain Gribble wrote that there was no going back. *The Japs had occupied my little fishing village but the rains had arrived and the track to the Hukawng was now as bad as those barbarous sons of Nippon. The country was rapidly becoming a bog, a quagmire.*

We set off about 7 a.m. The three muleteers were as stubborn as usual. Nobody could speak Yunnanese to them and their knowledge of Burmese was limited. However by 11 a.m. we were nearing the banks of the Tarung River. The sun was shining again and a shimmering haze hung between the trees. Horse flies buzzed about the necks and flanks of the mules. 'Topsy' (my pony) received constant attention from these flies and soon patches of blood began to show on her neck. Topsy was beginning to look thin. She was also suffering from a wound in the stifle the result of a kick from one of the mules. I walked alongside her and did my best to keep off the flies but it was an impossible task.

The first sign of the Tarung Hka was ghastly....I sent our mules a little way upstream to a village nearby. We would have to sleep in a Kachin house again that night if we were lucky.

I went down to the edge of the water, Lieutenant L came with me. Some bearded dusky-skinned men were trying to load a cart onto a raft while half a dozen of their comrades, armed with rifles, stood on guard. As we approached the scene, other armed refugees of another nationality, invaded the raft but were opposed by those already in possession. There was a terrific altercation and loaded rifles were thrust in all directions in an alarming manner. We rushed up to the raft expecting a local war to break out at any moment. Fortunately for us – and others – the raft could not support the combined weight of the contestants and began to sink, bringing the quarrel to an ignominious end.

The Kachin villagers were rendering invaluable assistance to the refugees ferrying them across this dangerous river. In the afternoon I met the local Akyiwa and elders and persuaded them to build two more rafts....They responded with enthusiasm.

MAY

Josephine was worried about the slow progress of her group and the fact that they had been told to cross the Chindwin river by the 15th. There were rumours that the Japanese were getting close. On May 14th they abandoned the rafts at midday and walked hard through afternoon, finding a PWD bungalow in which to sleep that night. There was another storm and the sole of her shoe was coming off.

On May 15th they walked early and reached the Chindwin river at 9 am. '*...Burma is very beautiful; the crystal clear river; the deep green jungle beyond; the purple-blue hills outlined clearly after the rain against the morning sky; the lights and shade of their curves and valleys..*' They must have met many other refugees on the way, and news was exchanged. They were told not to go to Homalin but to cross the river some miles to the south. They got country boats which were hollowed out tree trunks which could take five people.

Tonhe was yet another village crowded with evacuees, and with a school house standing empty. But inside were bodies of two cholera victims. They found space in another packed house, sheltered from the storm, and managed to acquire a tin of milk to add to their rice or tea. '*...We had dessert too, for the householder sold us a kind of sugar candy made from the toddy palm.*'

'...as you know if anyone dies in or under a house it has to be abandoned or the malignant Nats (spirits) will get us too...' **the Akyiwa's (headman's) wife**

Dr Russell's group were now travelling with the assistance of Maggie the elephant and her trained driver. *Friday May 15ᵗʰ dawned fine and clear. As I packed my few possessions in the early light a cuckoo called once and again in the near jungle. The sun rose, lighting with its level rays the mountain wall that seemed to bar our further path. Already many of the Indians had moved off, their carts at last abandoned, their bundles slung on the bullocks, or carried on their own backs. We swallowed a hasty meal. Ponies and elephant were loaded with our possessions. We picked up our haversacks and water-bottles and followed them down the winding track on the river bank. The plains of Burma lay behind us.*

Before us rose the Naga Hills. Beyond them lay safety. The path seemed never-ending. In the typical hill-track style it zig-zagged steeply up the mountain side, the thick jungle shutting out all but the rarest glimpses of the distant view. Before the long ascent had commenced for some distance we had clambered over the stones of the bed of a stream; then, as we left it, the heavens had opened, and the rain came down in sheets. The clay of the path rapidly became thick mud. And so slippery was the surface, that it was a matter of real difficulty to get round some of the steeper corners. Then, and on many occasions in the future we had to tackle them on hands and knees, with many falls..

Before our journey ended in Assam we were destined to learn a good deal about mud, of different qualities. During the frequent and torrential downpours the path became a rushing cataract of yellow water, each great footprint left by an elephant, a deep puddle. On the slopes it was difficult to stand; one looked desperately for any projecting root or stump against which to place the foot, or for any overhanging branch or bamboo by which to haul oneself up. The short and level area at the bottom of a dip was an unspeakable slough round which one picked a precarious way, if at all possible.

When the weather was fine the mud rapidly became a clay of the most remarkably glutinous kind. One learnt to sympathise heartily with a fly on a fly-paper! Every few steps the shoes were dragged off our heels, until in desperation we tried to bind them on with string or webbing cut from our haversacks. The continual drag on the shoe soon caused its disintegration. When I reached the end of the trek both heels had gone long before, and the soles of my shoes were only retained in place by such ligatures.

In the small collection of rough leaf-shelters dignified by the name of camps which were to be found every ten or a dozen miles, the mud assumed a different texture. There it was often black and always stinking. The site of each camp was indescribably fouled by the disgusting habits of many of our fellow-travellers. Every small stream near and every level stone on its banks was similarly polluted. Later in the march too in each camp there lay the unburied dead where they had dropped at last exhausted. As a result after the first day of our journey in the hills we found it impossible to stay the night in the regular camps, and preferred to build our own shelters, tired though we were, outside the area.

At the end of a gruelling march, a dish of tea was a wonderful restorative to the weary and rain-soaked traveller. Tea, generally without milk or sugar, drunk by the leaping flames of a fire that the advance guard had kindled, made the labours of the long day seem less formidable, the hills less steep. Some of our party, Gray, the trusty cook, the three Gurkha orderlies, always cheeful, revealed a rare skill in getting a fire going with soaking wood and rotten bamboo. It became the custom for some of the strongest walkers of the company to go ahead from the morning start, lightly burdened, in most cases to try and find suitable lodging for the night, and to light a fire. The system worked well in the early days, though later on as some of the less fit members grew weaker and travelled more and more slowly, there were serious disadvantages. Not once nor twice the rearguard found it impossible to overtake those in front, and one group or the other had to make camp without proper kit, wherever darkness and weariness overtook it in the jungle…

… A hill-top three thousand feet above our starting point was a wet and cold lodging for the first night. A sand-bank a few inches above the surface of a rapid stream was an island refuge for the second night: it was undoubtedly warmer, but quite as wet as that of the night before. As I waded upstream to our camp site carefully carrying my muddy shoes lest they get even wetter than they already were, a slippery stone proved my undoing, and - I took my evening bath! Clothes soon dry on one, fortunately, but sad to say the precious camera and films I was carrying with me went under as well, and water is not calculated to improve the quality of one's pictures: or so it proved, when the films were developed. (Despite this many of his remarkable photos survived.)

Before we lay down to sleep we carefully marked the level of the water lest the river rise during the night. On each side of the gorge, precipitous banks, thickly jungle-clad, rose towards the sky. The mists swirled round the tree-tops. With bamboos and leaves cut from the jungle we erected some sort of a shelter, but made the mistake of not sloping the roof steeply enough, so that it collapsed upon us when heavy and wet. It was a mistake we did not make twice! In the small hours, the rain descended upon us, speedily revealing the deficiencies of our shelter. But the dawn brought a fine sky, though dull and threatening, and we were able to move off in comparative dryness.

Old photo in the jungle (dml)

MAY

Captain Gribble had been having discussions with the local villagers. *May 15th Sixty Kachins appeared at an early hour. I went with them about half a mile away to the bamboo forest and before long they had felled a large number of bamboos. By 1 p.m. refugees were using the rafts.*

In the meantime tragedies occurred on the river. One old raft carrying a number of refugees broke up in the middle of the river and the wreckage, with its human cargo clinging to it, was swept away by the current and disappeared from sight! A dugout containing about 20 men capsized near the riverbank but all its passengers were saved. Some lost their bundles containing precious food.

All that day and far into the night the rafts and dugouts moved to and fro until the number of refugees on our side of the river was greatly reduced. I returned to rest with the most painful impression that the terrible defeatism I saw on all sides was due to a desperate food shortage, nor was there any certainty about getting supplies for many weary days to come.

May 16th Yawbang He got the mules and his pony safely across the river about a mile up-stream and set off for Shingbwiyang. *...It was an eerie procession tapering away into obscurity for nobody talked and many wore a scared or grim expression as if they were likely to be wandering about in this seemingly impenetrable forest until extinction. There were no villages to relieve the monotony and the track became foul with mud....The incidents on this part of the journey are too many and too sorrowful to record.....*

We arrived at Shingbwiyang at dusk.....The glow in the western sky lit up the outline of the hills – the Naga Hills – but the sight of them caused a stir of uneasiness for from now on the track would traverse those broken and precipitious forest-clad hills for one hundred miles or more!

...The Akyiwa's house built of bamboo and thatch was a long oblong, perhaps 100 feet long, with a projecting porch at each end. It stood on piles about five feet off the ground....With the exception of one or two old men, the house, presumably like the other six houses in the village, was entirely occupied by women and children, their men-folk having accompanied some of the earlier refugees in their endeavor to reach the Assam province of India. Four fires were blazing cheerfully on either side of the house as we entered, and dimly through the smoke I could see at either end of the long house some private apartments.

The Kachins and Nagas always welcomed Gribble and sought his advice. And there was a network of families who travelled through the jungle to bring him news. *I sat down at the nearest fire, while our blankets and food boxes were being untied and brought inside and slowly unfastened my puttees and boots, at the same time exchanging a greeting with the people of the house...."We feel safe now you are here." said the Akyiwa's wife, "but we cannot stay in the village. Listen to that dreadful noise below and in the porches at either end of the house. It goes on night and day. There are many sick among them and as you know if anyone dies in or under a house it has to be abandoned or the malignant Nats (spirits) will get us too...We women are terribly afraid and want to go away."...I said "You are very brave to have stayed here so long and I am quite certain you ought to remove your children and livestock." "Ningmoi village is less than two miles away: we will go there," she said.*

The little Naga woman, Ma Roi came to see him. He had met her on a previous visit to the forest....*I retired to my little apartment, livened up the fire and put my wet clothes round it. As I got under the blankets, who should walk in but the little Naga woman – Ma Roi. This time she was dressed in a long black and white striped frock, black socks and black patent leather shoes. She looked anxious, as if she had a lot to say, but I could not resist asking her how she obtained the English clothes. "From a European lady two weeks ago. She has since gone over the Naga Hills to India," Ma Roi answered. "She took a riding pony with her and many of the villagers too. My Uncle from Shingbwiyang, Tu Kawng went with her and she will be safe. But," she said impressively, "the monsoon weather has started and the rivers are rising. My cousin, the Duwa, is at Tagap Ga village, four days journey from here, but two of his men arrived last night to bring news to you."*

She told him of hundreds of refugees being held up at the Namyung river, and planes unable to drop supplies because of the weather: ..."*please hurry to Tagap Ga," she pleaded, "We will show you the way. All the rivers will soon be in flood, trees will be blown down, the track curling up and down the steep sides of the mountain will be obliterated." She concluded with great emphasis, "There are four big rivers to cross!". "The situation is becoming dreadfully complicated by the weather," I said to myself, "the outlook is horrible."*

He mentioned planes that were overhead dropping supplies. It was remarkable how many R.A.F planes managed this task. There would have been the constant threat of enemy aircraft, and they were flying over miles of impenetrable and monotonous jungle often covered with mist and rain clouds. The pilots had to fly through high mountain peaks and descend to within a few hundred feet to drop the loaded parachutes, often with very few landmarks to indicate the location of refugee camps.

May 17th ...How helpless we all felt and how envious we were that those gallant airmen would, in an hour or two, be back again among their colleagues on the right side of No-man's-land.....today the sun shone and the gleaming water in the river that skirted the village seemed so peaceful in the sunshine of that noonday that I was minded of my previous visit to this place only a few short months before when all was right with the world and God was in His heaven.   I had been privileged to see this place as it was, undisturbed by anything but the wildlife of the jungle.....I decided to go on the next day to Tagap Ga with such of the rations we still possessed.   I had never seen Tagap village but I knew it to be situated high up in the hills.   This thought reminded me of the two messengers waiting to see me....

CHAPTER FIFTEEN
May

'...My mind ran riot. "It was an astonishing situation," I thought, "In that fearful weather nobody could possibly continue the trek. Were we at the end of it?"...' **Captain Gribble**

Josephine's group had spent the night sheltering together with many other refugees in a house in the village of Tonhe. On May 16th she wrote: *'...We began the hard walk over the hills into India. It was a relief to be across the Chindwin because we were now going away from the Japanese instead of towards them. But we were still racing against time for the monsoon would break soon. Each day our programme was the same. At 5.30 we got up and drank plain tea, filled our bottles with boiled water and set out. We walked until 11.30 resting for five minutes each hour. At midday we ate our breakfast of boiled rice and then rested until 4. We walked again until 6 o'clock, had our evening meal of boiled rice and went to bed. On the first day the trek was rough and in hilly country, though there were no difficult climbs. May 17th Today we had a sheer climb for about three miles up a rocky mountainside. The cool breeze on the top was delicious and the view was grand, though clouds partly hid it.There were hospitable villagers in this district where we found houses for our midday meal and for shelter at night. Unfortunately they sheltered other living creatures too and it was not always possible to sleep. The nights were cold too. Our sack of rice was stolen, but a village headman sold us some more, and allowed us to shoot a small pig. We lived on pork for a day or two.*

Dr Russell had been drenched overnight, but in the morning there were breaks in the cloud and the sun would shine on the endless mountain peaks stretching far into the distance. Exhausting climbs lay ahead. *It was Sunday, the Sunday after Ascension, May 17th and as one surveys the whole trip, the worst day of them all. The path seemed to climb from dawn till dusk. the rain poured down nearly all day. The mud was worse than ever, and more slippery. Maggie, the elephant, was heavily laden, and at one time it seemed hopeless to expect her to struggle up those towering hills. When at last, as the light was going we reached the camp, we found it only a huddle of shelters already occupied on a hill-top 4000 ft high, across which a cold wind swept. Below the camp was a miserable trickle of muddy water, the only supply for the hundreds gathered there.*
*   Let us say no more about Nath Kaw, on its hill. It does not live in the*

memory as one of Burma's beauty spots. Adequately to describe it one would need a fire-proof typewriter and asbestos paper!

As we surmounted another crest next day, the weather began to improve. the clouds broke, and a watery sun shone across a mighty landscape. Below us, range after range for the most part densely wooded, rolled to the horizon. Here and there, each in its clearing, a small Naga village stood on a summit, or clung to some steep slope.

Old photo of part of Khumi Chin village   (dml)

Far below, still hidden in its narrow valley, and ten miles away, rushed the Namyung river, name of evil omen to the refugee. Two thousand feet beneath us a cluster of tiny huts marked our immediate destination, the village of Tagap.

Wilfred Crittle wrote: '*...By this time distress among the refugees was becoming acute and many had been without food for two or three days. While resting on the side of the road I saw Amah Singh, one of the oldest Sikh inhabitants of Kamaing. He was walking very slowly with the aid of a bamboo. When he saw me he stopped and begged for something to eat. "Only half a biscuit, Sahib, only half a biscuit." I am sure that he did not believe me when I told him I hadn't got half a biscuit in the world....*'

Josephine too was often drenched and travelling through mountainous countryside. *May 18th   The rains broke, but we walked doggedly on.*

STORIES OF SURVIVAL IN BURMA

At midday we reached a village where we hoped to have breakfast and dry our clothes, but some British soldiers there told us to move on as quickly as we could. 'We have a case of cholera in this hut.' We spent a bitterly cold night in a draughty house at the height of 4000 feet. May 19th We met some more military folk in a village. One of them had just died of cholera through drinking river water two days before....I had done that twice since I left Katha when I was hot and had had no boiled water left in my bottle. My shoes could stand no more, and I left them on the wayside. An Irrawaddy Flotilla Company captain gave me his spare pair, size 8 - a little large. We heard that Imphal had been bombed either once or twice....trekking out of the war into it. The jungle had its trials, but at least it was free from bombs and machine guns. As we ate our evening meal of boiled rice and tea, we indulged the animal man by discussing what we should eat first when we got to Calcutta. I chose chocolate and cheese, a pound of each to begin with would do.

Dr Russell had glimpsed the village of Tagap, 2000 feet below. *Descending the long hill there came to us the distant hum of a plane. Once again succour from the sky was at hand. A big transport aircraft swept into view over the hills, and began to circle above the village. Parachutes broke from it and dropped slowly to the ground. From our view-point, high on the mountain-side we had the unusual experience of seeing plane and parachutes far below us. For the first time in our lives we found ourselves looking down on the R.A.F.!*
In the middle of the village our advance-guard met us with the cheering news that they had secured an empty Naga hut with a sound roof and a share of the rations recently dropped from the sky. Gladly we climbed the notched log that gave access to the interior, and took possession of our temporary home. A welcome fire burnt in the middle of the hut. Soon a remarkable array of wet garments hung round it and festooned the walls. Outside the sky clouded over again, and the rain swept across the hills. It streamed from the thick thatch and gurgled into the water-bottles placed underneath. We stretched tired limbs on the bamboo floor. Let it rain!

Captain Gribble was also heading for the village of Tagap Ga which meant he was now further north than he usually went on his routine expeditions into the jungle. With the animals and the three muleteers they pressed on through the forest. A day or two after Dr Russell's group they reached Nathkaw. *May 18th, 19th, and 20th – Jungle*

MAY

Camps ....the track became more and more uneven, irregular, broken as a choppy sea....We then began an ascent up the side of a mountain that seemed to be never ending ... If it had been possible to ask refugees at the start of the trek to name the greatest dangers of the tropical forest they would most probably have referred to savages, wild beasts and snakes. Savages there were none and but for the invaluable help rendered by the Kachin and Naga villagers the list of tragedies would indeed have been far longer. Wild beasts were as scared of the refugees as the latter were of the jungle. In that wealth of trees it was at times hard to find water and throats became parched. Dystentery, malaria and exhaustion began to take a heavy toll...We pitched camp for the first night on the side of a ridge, which the two Nagas who accompanied us called Kying-lao. We built ourselves a little shelter and made the best of a bad night...we spent the second night on a mountain, which the Nagas call Nathkaw, 4000 feet above sea level!

The third day of the trek from Shingbwiyang was again in pouring rain and the track was churned up with mud......Presently a batch of 30 Kachins passed us going in the opposite direction. They marched in single file....They exchanged greetings with Ningru who was walking along behind me, but did not stop. Ningru told me they were returning from the Namyung Hka after assisting refugees......because they had run out of food. When I asked Ningru if the Kachins said anything about the track ahead he looked glum.

Ningru spoke of crowds of people at the villages and rivers.... *"Most of the Nagas have deserted their village and it is quite impossible to get food and the river is a raging torrent....It is too late to reach the Assam frontier and I shall have to return to my village or starve to death."*

...The two Nagas and Ma Roi were the only three persons who seemed unconcerned. In these wretched conditions they were able to get along faster than any one and at times seemed to show a slight impatience at our slow progress. From time to time I made an effort to chat with them. The two young men were shy but Ma Roi made up for what they lacked in chatter. She was wearing an old khaki sun-hat and the striped frock, but her feet were now bare...At times she seemed to bound ahead and then wait until her two friends caught her up when she would greet them with a smile and spring forward again.....I questioned them on the news I had received that morning from Ningru. What was going to happen to all those people trapped at the river crossing at Namyung Hka?

Kyun Dao described the planes dropping supplies which had then stopped coming because of the weather. Some Naga villagers had sold the contents to the refugees. ... *"Why did the villagers sell what did not belong to them?" I asked. "Because our gardens were uprooted and our livestock looted," Kyun Dao replied. "Now most of the villagers have gone to their field huts on the hillsides and have built spiked bamboo stockades round the maize and millet crops. They will remain there and guard the fields. If we do not take such precautions we too shall starve. Many of the refugees have died and their bodies lie in the jungle all round Tagap village.....even if they cross the Namyung Hka there are three more large rivers beyond. Every day it rains and the rivers get deeper and fiercer."*

Ma Roi who had been listening to our conversation then said light-heartedly, "You need not worry for we will look after you during the rainy season, build you a house and share with you our food." I smiled at this, but was to learn later that it was no idle remark and that without the help of these kindly Naga people I should not be writing this story.

After crossing the Nathkaw ridge the violence of the rain increased and was accompanied by a high searching wind. The water streamed from heaven and forest and seemed to laugh at us and chase us down the precipitous curling slopes in the direction of Tagap Ga. The air was a greyness of melting and swiftly moving cloud. 'If it rains like this it must rain itself out before long." I thought, but I was wrong for it even increased until the earth ran water and the air seemed liquid. How anyone succeeded in wading through that dreadful morass to Tagap Ga I really don't know. Refugees continually fell or slipped down the steep incline and a great many were coated with yellow mud from head to foot.

We had been staggering along since 7 a.m. without a pause and I was beginning to feel very depressed at this unending ghastly journey when suddenly about 2 p.m. I saw to the right of the track the outline of a long Naga house looming out of the mist. Kyun Dao touched me on the wrist, "That is the Akyiwa's house in Upper Tagap, Naga village and all are crowded with refugees and every day sees them increase. The lower village is about 11 miles further down the ridge. It contains eleven houses all occupied by refugees. The villagers have run away with their women and children to their field-huts."

We moved away from the track to the long house in front of us. R and I were the first to arrive. We climbed the 'ladder' (the trunk of a tree with notches cut in it at intervals) and stepped on to the front veranda. It was closed on three sides but open at the end, which overlooked the cloud-ridden valley below.... The three young Nagas disappeared into the dark interior of the house. In a few minutes they reappeared with a tall and immensely strong looking man – the owner of the house. He wore a tartan skirt checked with green, yellow and red colours – distinctive of the hill clans – and a black jacket. I tried to read in his dark pockmarked face the kind of impression our bedraggled appearance made on him but I could discover nothing but sympathetic interest in our deplorable condition. He greeted us with a smile....."Some wood will be brought to make a fire. The monsoon is violent and it shows no sign of abating. I will go and call the Duwa who wants to see you."

A group of refugees arrived including 'the Padre', which may have been Dr Russell's party. Tea was made. Gribble continued:....*As we were swallowing the hot liquid a stocky figure of a man appeared in the doorway and limped towards me. It was the Duwa, with whom I had discussed smugglers not so long ago.* The Naga chief was calm and hospitable towards Gribble and sought his advice. But he spoke of great fear amongst his people of the refugees who in some cases were driven by desperation to violent behaviour.

Gribble was beginning to feel overwhelmed by the situation. ...*In my anxiety and helplessness I was indeed more than glad to see him. He did not appear to be in the least perturbed. No shadow of mistrust showed in his dark brown eyes. He greeted me and suggested that I should accompany him to an inner room where we could talk with less likelihood of interruption........I began to realize that the space below the house, ordinarily used for cattle, pigs, dogs and fowls was crowded with humanity. There were cries of children, the coughing and groaning of men and women – a veritable bedlam. We walked into the porch and I peered under the house. It was a terrible pathetic sight. ..."Every house is the same," said Sambaw, "crowded with refugees, inside, outside and underneath. So far we have managed to prevent them from entering this house by barring the door but their numbers are increasing every minute. What will we do?" "You will not be able to keep them out," I replied. "They are short of food, tired and consequently frightfully difficult to cope with."*

We entered a very dark room and it was some moments before I could see the other occupants. The room contained more than a dozen Nagas together with two or three of their women including Ma Roi. I sat on the floor near the fire and listened to their chatter. I could not understand the Naga dialect and asked them what it was all about. Sambaw explained in the Kachin dialect that the villagers were terribly afraid of the bands of armed men among the refugees. The villagers who remained behind at his request wanted to clear off to their field huts. They had barely enough rice for themselves but some of the scanty stocks hidden here and there had been discovered and seized by gangs of looters…… I asked the Duwa to explain to the villagers not to be afraid, that there was much to be done and their assistance was necessary. I would meet them all again early next morning.

Gribble returned to the other group and ate with them. Later he could not sleep. *My mind ran riot. "It was an astonishing situation," I thought, "In that fearful weather nobody could possibly continue the trek. Were we at the end of it?" For many of these lost souls the answer was already plain. I suddenly sat up on the floor. The wailing of children in the space below was nerve-wracking….It was like the legendary entrances into hell. I lay down again feeling a little sick. Presently some sort of peace came over the house and I fell into an exhausted sleep.*

CHAPTER SIXTEEN
May

'... *"The Duwa sees no hope of the refugees being able to get across the Namyung Hka for months to come."...'* **Ma Roi**

For the moment Dr Russell's group were unable to move on. ...*Like the mists that curled over the hill-side, the rumour was slight and vague at first; soon it strengthened into dark certainty. The Namyung Hka in its gorge five miles away had risen many feet and was impassable. A few hours before little more than ankle deep, storms in the high hills had swept down, and now it ran nearly shoulder-high over its rocky bed, a formidable torrent that even an elephant dared not face.*

An envoy from the party volunteered to undertake the long march down to the ford and back to bring news of the situation. Pearson it was who returned, wet and weary in the late afternoon, to tell of the wide and rushing river and of the hundreds trying in vain to cross. We heard of desperate attempts with flimsy bamboo rafts, of men swept away and rescued with difficulty, of some who perished in the waters. It was clear that we should have to wait until the torrent abated; how long that would be nobody could tell.

To the crowded village on its narrow hill-top the planes once more brought badly needed supplies that Tuesday morning, May 19th . One pilot skilfully dropped most of his load in or near the huts and the bags were gathered into a big pile under the guard of our party. Another pilot however was less fortunate, and we saw with chagrin and dismay parachutes and sacks dropping far off into the jungle on the lower slopes were no one could hope to find them.

After this promising start however the clouds covered our hill-top eyrie, and the planes came no more during our stay of four days. On the Thursday indeed we heard our friends above trying to pierce the blanket of mist that hid us, but in vain. A few minutes after they had given up the attempt that meant so much to the starving folk below the sky cleared but they had returned to their far-off bases. We pictured the pilots sitting down to lunch, perhaps with the resolve to try again next day: but that picture did little to fill empty bellies!

On one or two of the boxes of stores we opened we found messages of encouragement pencilled by those who had loaded them into the planes on some Assam aerodrome. To read: "Good Luck!" or "We deliver the goods!" warmed the heart.

There were stories of the difficulties of distributing the limited supplies fairly to desperate people, and of having none left when yet more travellers came to the village.   What they couldn't have known was the huge effort required in organising these food supplies. In Assam there was a shortage of many things including foodstuffs, parachutes and food containers. Great care had to be taken packing the food, with an outer sack loosely holding two inner sacks that would probably burst on impact with the ground. Inevitably some containers were lost in the jungle, and there were tragic cases of people being injured or even killed when hit by a box falling from a plane.

Dr Russell wrote: *One of the parachutes had not finished its career of usefulness when the goods had been delivered.   Its cords, cut off served a variety of purposes, lashing bundles to pack-ponies, repairing shoes, even assisting at the birth of a baby!   The fabric divided between three of four chilly mortals helped to keep us warm at night.   Undoubtedly we owe a tremendous debt of gratitude to the men of the R.A.F. who strove to save the lives of the refugees from Burma.*

As the number reaching the village increased, so too did the number of sick and dying.   Drugs were scarce, more especially owing to an unfortunate mischance, by which my chief medical box had been carried past the village. On the morning of our arrival in it, we had availed ourselves of an offer of help by a party travelling with several elephants, and placed some of our kit upon their beasts, the medical box included. This party, being enabled to travel faster than ours, had reached and crossed the Namyung River before it rose;   our goods went with it, and we did not recover them for a whole week.   Again and again one had to tell the sick who came to our hut that there were no drugs available for their particular complaint.   Without the tools of his trade, a doctor is a singularly useless being, nor is he particularly ornamental! It would surely have been justifiable to act upon the apostolic injunction, and deprive the 'Doc.' of his share of the meagre rations!

One rather macabre incident lives in the memory.   With the help of Rushton (who was indefatigable in the public weal) and two very unwilling coolies, I was removing the two-day-old corpse of an unfortunate traveller from under the hut where his journey had ended. As I lifted the shoulders on to an improvised stretcher a bullock standing behind swished the side of my face with its tail.   For a heart-stopping second, I thought the silent figure had raised its hand to stop me from disturbing its last sleep!

MAY

Josephine's group were climbing high mountains and heading for Imphal which they had heard had been bombed. These were probably the last weeks when the military and many other refugees were able to travel on this particular route to the west. On May 20th they set out with raincoats wrapped around their kit to keep blankets dry and covered seventeen miles. Josephine had no warm clothes with her. '...*But it was grand country and never before have I been among such lively, fast-moving clouds, now filling the valleys, now hiding the hills. How the wind blew! I hurried because I was so cold..... 'Stop this wind and this rain, I can't bear it and I am freezing right through' - I offered the Almighty a very childish prayer. And then I laughed to think that I should expect God to change the course of the monsoon because one insignificant mortal was chilly in the hills. 'All the same,' I went on, 'You could give me some warmth from inside myself, couldn't You?'*

Her account moves on rapidly at this point. Compared to Dr Russell's group they appear to have covered the miles in a short number of days, or possibly some details were not recorded or were written later from memory. *At a fork in the path a notice on a tree pointed to the right. 'To India' it said. The highway to India, two feet wide and six inches deep in mud. We took the road to India, a steep winding descent of three miles into the valley.*

The path was now more like a rushing stream. We reached the village at midday and found tinned provisions for evacuees and a hospitable villager who lent us his house; one large room with a blazing fire in the middle of the floor. We got warm and dry.

In the late afternoon we went on for a few miles. We were now in Manipur State and at dusk we reached a village of high caste Hindus. We had to pay heavily for permission to sleep on the verandah of the village granary. But it was the cleanest village I have ever seen in the East; as neat and trim and as well laid out as an English suburban housing estate. May 21st. A few miles from the Manipuri village we reached a road and Yaripuk where we had a good meal in the PWD bungalow. We went by lorry to Imphal. It was more or less deserted except for the military.

Captain Gribble was still in the village of Tagap Ga, high in the hills.
May 21st Today is as cold and wet as a sea fog. The mules, born and bred in the plains, whinnied their distress....The three muleteers were quite unconcerned about the animals and had ensconced themselves in a little dark room in the house where they settled down and forgot the

outside world in their insensate craving for opium... He described the day with more and more refugees arriving, more sickness and death. They did not attempt to move on. *...Presently Ningru came along and told me he had shifted my bedding and his own to a small room inside the house which the Akyiwa pointed out to him....* A Naga presented Gribble with two cobs of Indian corn and a pumpkin. *...Ma Roi appeared with an armful of firewood and straight away kindled a fire.*

She was now dressed in her native costume and looked more becoming. As usual she was full of chatter. She said, "The Duwa sees no hope of the refugees being able to get across the Namyung Hka for months to come. It is now a yellow torrent and nobody can cross. The aeroplanes cannot come and drop food and he does not know what will happen to the mass of refugees. He has sent messages to the other chiefs to come and meet you here but they are afraid of the river and cannot come."

"How terribly pessimistic are the Nagas," I thought, but I answered her as cheerfully as I could and said, "I expect the weather will clear up in a day or two and everybody can cross the river. What we want is a rope." "The Duwa thinks we have a chance of getting across the Tarung Hka and going to his village which is on the ridge opposite here. You can meet the other chiefs there and talk to them about the refugees. The Duwa also says that this village and the lower villages have now become 'villages of death' and no one can live in them again. The houses must be burned down."

I said, "I have arranged with the Duwa to visit the lower village tomorrow and see what is happening there when I come back we will decide what to do." "The other village is down there," she said, pointing downwards, "and the track is deep in mud. He will take you by another path." As she went out she added, "We have been discussing everything in another room and all of us, men and women want to get away from here. We shall be safe in the Duwa's village which can be easily reached in one day." It was quite evident from this conversation that although Ma Roi was a woman she had quite a lot to say in the councils of the elders!

....It was a terrible night and I hardly knew what sustained us. Incidents were so many that it was impossible to appreciate them or quicken our sympathies. Perhaps our minds were dazed and our hearts hardened to the grim realities around us....Everyone instinctively realized that rain or no rain, mud or no mud, somehow or other it was necessary to get across that river or perish in the attempt. To sit still was fatal. A few

bullocks and mules would not, without Divine Aid go very far with that hungry multitude.

Dr Russell's group were also considering the prospect of trying to cross the raging Namyung River, and at this critical time there was an unwelcome dispute about the elephant. In his party were soldiers who had already been in a weakened state when they had begun the journey back in April.

Perhaps, by some standards her looks would not have taken a prize, but if handsome is as handsome does she was a regular killer! Admittedly she was on the heavy side, and broad to boot. She must have turned the scale at 6,000 lbs, and stood seven and a half feet high at the shoulder! You see, we are not thinking of any mysterious uncrowned queen of the Naga Hills, but Maggie, our faithful elephant! From Shinbwiyang with her Jingpaw mahout, she had carried a heavy load of kit and stores over some of the worst paths imaginable. Now her future and ours was dark. The mahout flatly refused to go any farther. True he had only agreed to come as far as the Namyung, but we hoped all along that further persuasion, and further bribes might cause him to change his mind. But it was all in vain. Rushton pleaded with him for hour after hour, in Jingpaw, I weighed in with Burmese. We stressed the needs of our convalescents, and their inability to carry loads on those fearful paths. We even showed him the terrible scars of one of our party in proof of what we said: that undoubtedly caused him to waver, but only for a minute.

Before the mahout drew his wages, and took his departure back to his village in the Hukawng, he handed over the elephant to us and taught us the words of command which rule the actions of the great beast. We were determined to do our best to drive her ourselves, and once on the march so equable was her temperament we had good hopes of success. But the real difficulty was the finding of Maggie in the early morning. According to the usual custom, she was hobbled with a dragging chain at night, and turned loose to graze. It is impossible to tie up and feed with cut fodder, a beast that consumes bamboo shoots by the hundredweight. The first duty of the mahout at crack of dawn is to follow the tracks of elephant and chain through the soaking jungle, up hill and down dale, sometimes for miles, until he finds and brings back his mighty charge.

The situation seemed hopeless. But as in the past, God, Who knew our need, fully supplied it. Our prayers were answered and that remarkably. There came into the village on the twentieth evening two members of the Information Bureau who had been resident in Siam for many years. With them there travelled a Burman, a skilled mahout and owner of elephants. He agreed to drive and ride Maggie into Assam, if we in our turn undertook to carry the kit of the little party in the elephant's basket and help them with rations. Both parties were more than satisfied with the arrangement. Our transport was secured, our greatest anxiety was at an end.

It was obvious that when the river was low enough we should be able to cross with the aid of the elephant, but what of the people who should come after? If we could stretch a rope across the ford and leave it in place it would prove a great help to all who had to wade. Though all the inhabitants of the village had fled when the first of the refugees appeared in their neighbourhood, two or three re-visited their homes and told us that there was abundant cane to be had in the jungles high up on the mountain-side. The next day, Thursday 21ˢᵗ therefore Rushton with the elephant spent many hours climbing the hill in order to drag from the trees the cane needed to make a rope. But as we so often found, Naga miles are elastic, and our leader found it necessary to return empty-handed, lest he be benighted in the jungle. By ransacking every house in the village however, enough rope was collected to stretch across the river when we reached it.

From time to time throughout the day, a sudden burst of rifle-fire resounded from the jungle round the village. It did not portend the arrival of a Jap detachment but merely the appearance of some small and frightened porker, the property of a luckless Naga. To the hungry travellers the sight of fresh meat 'on the trotter' was too great a temptation to be resisted. One such trophy of the chase fell to the guns of our party, but, with a rush of honesty unusual in those parts, we paid the owner Rs. 5/-, when we got into touch with him. Our three Gurhas in high glee roasted the little carcase over the fire, and bits of pork were passed round our hut that night about 11 p.m. Those who were bold enough to sample it pronounced it tough but tasty. They appeared to sleep quite well after the feast, too!

Many of the nights in Tagap, and on the march, were made very unpleasant by the advent after dark of swarms of tiny black 'sand-flies' which bit like red-hot needles. What their scientific name was I do not know; what we called them is neither here nor there! They were small enough to romp through the meshes of an ordinary mosquito net, four abreast and laughing heartily. A sand-fly net kept them at bay on most occasions, but even that failed some nights. They got under a blanket, and inside a shirt. The night was their best hunting time, but on the hills they were never altogether absent. A minute's pause for a breather on the march was certain to produce several fiery bites on legs or arms: it was a decided stimulus to press onward.

The Naga hut in which we spent those four days at Tagap is perhaps worthy of description. Long, low and thatched, it stood on posts five feet from the ground. The front half opened on a veranda, the full width of the hut from which the eye swept a fine view of tumbled hills. In the middle of the floor stood an earth-filled hearth, and round the fire at night slept most of our party, packed together like slabs in a parquet floor. Behind this main room was a much smaller compartment lacking any window to the outside; another fire in here filled most of the available space. A wide passage ran from the front room to a narrow back veranda from which we distributed any spare stores we had. Down both sides of the hut outside the walls but still under the eaves, ran narrow verandas about two feet wide. Their purpose was to prevent the thrusting of a spear into the hut by any nocturnal enemy. On the walls hung a few skulls, not the human ones so many expected; they were nothing more fearful than those of monkeys, slain in the chase. It seems perhaps a pity to dispel so pleasantly horrifying an illusion, but it must be pointed out that the Nagas in these ranges have not hunted heads for many a long year. There are Nagas who still indulge in this very anti-social and unfriendly hobby, but their territory lies many miles away.

Let it not be thought that this commodious residence was exclusively reserved for our use. Every available foot of space beneath our floor was occupied by fellow-travellers, and the smoke of their little fires, the smell of their cooking, (when they had anything to cook) rose to our nostrils, but not like incense. All along the side verandas slept others at night. When a baby cried, we all shared the maternal wakefulness: when someone snored, we all displayed the same desire to tell him about it.

Friday morning dawned fine. It was obvious that the Namyung Hka must have fallen somewhat, for there had been little heavy rain for the past forty-eight hours. An advance party sent back word that such indeed was the case. Food was running very short. It was essential that we push on if at all possible. Maggie was brought to the veranda; our kit was loaded on her back. The sun was past the meridian when we bade farewell to 'Hill-Top Hotel' and turned our backs upon Tagap.

CHAPTER SEVENTEEN
May

'...the path in front was dangerously undercut, and her wonderful instinct told her it might not sustain her three tons of weight...' **Dr Russell**

Dr Russell's group set out again. *After a short rise, in the middle of which lay a corpse, many days old – and every mile or two brought a similar grim reminder of our own precarious hold upon life – the path descended steeply to the Namyung valley. Halfway down, under a clump of bamboos on the hillside and a few yards from the path, I found an anxious father supporting a groaning woman, and two small children howling by her side. A brief enquiry elicited the fact that the poor family had been on the move from far-away Lashio, and that the third member had decided to enter this unfriendly world at a most inopportune time! In place of sterile scissors my rusty pocket-knife; for ligatures, a piece of parachute cord from my haversack; as restorative, a drink of stale rainwater from my water-bottle, and the population of the Naga hills had been increased by the arrival of a fine baby girl! The next day I saw the mother apparently none the worse for her experience down by the river, and we were able to give her a lift across on the elephant.*

In the valley bottom the narrow path followed the river climbing and dipping, as it meandered towards the ford. As we rounded one corner we were dismayed to see Maggie's vast hindquarters backing in our direction from behind a projecting rock. The path turned sharply, cutting into the hillside to cross a side stream, and Maggie refused to trust her considerable bulk to the next few yards. Again and again the mahout urged her to it, hammering on her obstinate head with his dah, or short sword, until the blade flew from the handle and flew clanging down into the stream. Luckily I was able to spot it lying on the stones, and by lowering myself into the thick vegetation succeeded in retrieving it. But all efforts were vain, the elephant declined to proceed. We unloaded all the kit on to the side of the track, and even removed the basket. Still nothing would persuade her ladyship to go round the corner. As later inspection revealed, she was undoubtedly right in her obstinacy: the path in front was dangerously undercut, and her wonderful instinct told her it might not sustain her three tons of weight.

It looked like the end of our transport. With a heavy heart I went on to call the rest of the party back, to hump the kit on to the ford. As I returned to the place half an hour later to my surprise and delight I found Maggie, with her mahout climbing back on to the path below the dangerous spot.

The skilful driver had managed to get her to crash a way down the almost precipitous bank, jungle-covered, right into the river below. Thence she had walked upstream a short distance, and climbed up again to the track above. It did not take long to carry the basket, heavy cane harness, chains, and baggage past the bad bit, and re-load the elephant. With thankful hearts we followed her down the hill to the camp site.

Josephine had reached India and experienced the support and hospitality of the Teaplanters. On May 22nd in pouring rain they went 133 miles by lorry from Imphal to Manipur Road railway station, a narrow winding road crossing the hills at nearly 6000 feet. '*...We arrived at 8 pm and had dinner in the Teaplanters' camp. So civilised and clean and comfortable.*

Captain Gribble's group struggled down towards the lower village of Tagap. *May 22nd ...We followed a very steep precipitous trail which at one time had been a mule track leading to the river below. It was now a sloping track of thick sticky mud which refugees tried to avoid by clinging to bushes and branches of trees but into which they continually fell....*

...For nearly two hours we ploughed our way down this nightmare trail sometimes in mud and frequently in water until, through the mist and rain we came in sight of the lower village. And what a ghastly sight it was, incredible, unbelievable. Here in the heart of the Naga Hills surrounded by impenetrable jungle, in pouring rain and with little or no food, was a mass of people jammed in and under the primitive Naga huts. Indian, Chinese and European, soldiers, civilians, 'purdah' women and children, Anglo-Indians, men and women, old and young alike all huddled together, thoroughly miserable, fearful of the immediate future.

Padre Crittle went in search of the river which he hoped to locate somewhere in the misty valley below. I wandered round the village. Search parties were sent into the jungle to hunt for food which had missed the village and dropped in the jungle. But the weather must improve rapidly and the river become fordable in order to save these unhappy people...

Gribble speculated about rope, a bridge he had heard was going to be constructed over the Namyung Hka, the possibility of a break in the weather and the hope of more help from supply planes *...These thoughts heartened me and I said as much to some men I spoke to. "We will keep a sharp look out, they said, "and make every effort to recover all that is* *dropped from the air as soon as the weather improves."*

He made his way back to the upper village guided along a better track by a Naga villager. At this point he was plagued by indecision about what to do next. ....*The Padre returned soon afterwards.....He said the depth of the river was breast high but dropping. He thought it might be possible to cross the next day and as rations were short he wanted to continue the journey.*

That night I came to a decision. The other members of my group could go on to the river but I would stay with the Nagas, so long as it was feasible to do so. I felt that the Duwa and his villagers would be loyal even if the worst were to happen and I was forced to stay among them until the end of the rains...

May 23ʳᵈ The unexpected happened. It was a fine day and for the first time I was able to get a long view of the mountainous forest-clad country. From the veranda of the Akyiwa's house the wooded folds of the mountains fell steeply away into the valley concealed in the mist below....

All that morning the refugees streamed away into the jungle and by midday only the sick and the moribund remained behind. But more half-starved weary people began to arrive during the afternoon from the high ridge behind us. "Strange," I thought, "why aircraft do not drop food-packets in this upper village."

We put out signals and lighted fires but it was not till late in the afternoon that two planes came over and released parachutes from which were suspended some wooden boxes....At dusk, Padre Crittle expressed his desire to go next morning and join the other missionaries, and try to get across the Namyung Hka. I agreed to go with the Padre. G undertook to escort some women, and take the few surviving mules. My Indian companion, Dr Roi chose to sink or swim with me. I felt heartened by his devotion. Ningru Nawng who had come with me from Kamaing now decided to try and get back to his home in the Kachin Hills. I would miss him greatly for he had been a staunch and faithful follower.

Tonight we divided our scanty food supply and turned in early....Many people had died on the slopes of the Ngalang ridge, about half way from here to the Pass. I looked at my map, it showed the Ngalang ridge to be 5000 feet elevation.

Dr Russell's group were preparing to try and cross the dangerous Namyung Hka. They still had their elephant who had descended a slippery precipitous slope into the river and emerged again. *The night before we attempted the crossing was spent in a group of shelters which rose like islands from a sea of unusually black and stinking mud. It seemed really a waste of time to go down to the edge of the river and endeavour to wash off the worst of the day's dirt; one was sure to be plentifully befouled again returning to the camp! But to remove in the rushing water the pounds of clay that transformed shoes and socks into unrecognizable masses did at least make for ease in putting them on again next morning. One of the outstanding horrors of a march such as ours was the loathesome business, daily repeated, of dragging on wet footwear in the cold light of dawn. Many a pair of socks came to an untimely end by fire because the owner hung them up to dry at night over the camp fire and forgot them until the morning. But by this stage in any case, few of our socks boasted toes or heels: they were, literally, anklet socks!*

Near our camp in a miserable little shelter I found two unfortunate Chinese soldiers, wounded and left by their comrades. The smell of their wounds polluted the air around. They had apparently no food. One of them came to our fireside and in return for a little bully-beef timidly proffered a five rupee note. We told him to keep his money: what was the use of it, anyhow?

Together with hundreds of others we gathered on the steep bank of the Namyung Hka on Saturday morning, May 23rd. The river ran swiftly in its gorge more than a hundred yards wide. On both sides the tree-clad hills rose towards the sky. Across the water an acre of flat ground was covered with leaf shelters. Similar rough huts were clustered amoung the trees behind us. Though it was still falling the river rose waist-high on me, a good four feet. So strong was the current and so rough the bed that no women and few men could stand against it unaided. As we watched group after group clinging to a long bamboo struggled across to the opposite bank and climbed wearily up to dry ground. This was to prove Maggie's finest hour. Loaded with women, with kit, with men too, she strode through the rushing waters, ever returning for another burden. With her aid we stretched the cane rope from bank to bank, but it was not as much use as had been hoped. On our side the bank was high, and there was no convenient tree by the water's edge to which to make it fast. As a result, those who sought to cross by its aid could not reach it until well out into the current. But in spite of that it was instrumental in saving lives. An Indian, wading the stream higher up, lost his footing and was swept down. Clutching the rope despairingly as he passed, he hung on, the water dashing over his head and shoulders.

Rushton and another waded out and tried to get him to turn upstream, and to drop the heavy water-logged bundle to which he still clung. But fear had chased his senses away, and commands passed over his head like the waves. His burden dragged off and flung away sharp blows brought him to himself, and he was safely brought back to the bank. Another man, an English soldier, also slipped, and was carried down stream, snatching at the rope but missing it. It was a fine sight to see George Tidey race after him with a powerful crawl stroke, overtake him and draw him to the shelter of the bank again.

Maggie too did her bit at life-saving. A group of people, including several women were in difficulties in mid-stream, and were at the point of exhaustion. The mahout seeing their plight, with great presence of mind brought the elephant alongside them, and they, using her great bulk as a backwater, were able to struggle to safety.

(sfr)

MAY

It was time I crossed. Removing everything but shorts and shoes, I passed clothing, wrist-watch, glasses and the rest to one of our party who was crossing on Maggie's back.. Then with Tidey and three other men, we gripped a bamboo eight feet long, and waded into the river. The current buffeted us. In mid-stream my foot slipped, I was spun round, and went under, but clung fiercely to the bamboo, and was able to struggle to my feet again. A minute later, Tidey also took a ducking, but after further strenuous efforts we found ourselves, to our great relief, nearing the far bank, and thankfully dragged ourselves up into the overhanging bushes. We were over!

Whilst we wrung the water from our nether garments I watched with considerable anxiety two of our party crossing singly, each with a stick. They were making heavy weather of it and came to a standstill in the middle, leaning against the current. One of them had to be rescued by the elephant, but Pearson gallantly struggled on and reached safety.

For many hours that day Rushton, indefatigable where there was work to be done stood at the water's edge and helped those he selected into the basket on Maggie's back. Had he been commercially minded he could have been much richer for his day's work. Wealthy Indians were offering him Rs. 1,000/- for the trip across, but the only qualification was helplessness; all others had to wade, or wait until the river sank further.

The last trip of the day brought over three Anglo-Indian girls, an old Indian chemist from the factory at Sahmaw, and his plump little boy. I went across with the mahout to pick up these particular passengers at the urgent request of our Sahmaw friends who had just come over. One had to harden one's heart to the clamour of entreaty that went up from the crowds still waiting on the bank. The small boy whom we picked up was grossly and helplessly fat: he hung like a balloon on the elephant's side, while I strove desperately to haul him up into the basket by the arms. Kicking out aimlessly he caught his doting parent a shrewd blow in the face. At last by main force we got him up, and heavily loaded our noble elephant almost exhausted, crossed the river for the last time.

A mile from the scene of these labours we found a very steep but dry clearing, and there we camped for the night. Soon other parties joined us, our friends from Sahmaw and Namti. Shelters were erected, fires twinkled through the dusk. We supped, more lightly than we should have liked, and laid our weary frames upon the remarkably unyielding bosom of Mother Earth.

STORIES OF SURVIVAL IN BURMA

(sfr)

CHAPTER EIGHTEEN
May

Calcutta: '….*famine, high prices and overcrowding, with flies innumerable, and heat almost past bearing….' Dr Russell*

Josephine wrote: *May 23rd   At 5 am we started the long journey on the train to Calcutta.*

Later on Dr Russell wrote: *'Proud was the title borne by Calcutta, that teeming human rabbit-warren which sprawls along the banks of the muddy Hooghly river.   Before this war mention of its name called forth, in the minds of most people, an association with the notorious "Black Hole" from the times of Clive in India and the Nawab of Bengal in 1756.*

But for others will be the recollection that many will carry away, who have been brought to India as the results of Japanese aggression.   Men and women of the Burma Campaign who came from the villages of Britain, or the wide plains and great cities of the United States, from Chungking, Lagos or Mombasa.

These will surely associate Calcutta with dirt indescribable and foul disease.   With famine, high prices and overcrowding, with flies innumerable,   and   heat   almost   past   bearing…..To   this   great conglomeration of human beings the train brought the family, whose fortunes we follow.

Muriel and her children lived for a time in a hostel. '…*At night a large friendly rat emerged from a drain in the bathroom, and passed through the bedroom on his foraging expeditions to the house beyond.   So well established did it consider its right of way, it used to scratch and snuffle at the door demanding admission.*

There were also other but smaller visitants who made their prescence felt at night.   These bed-bugs looked like lady-birds, but instead of "flying away home" left their mark in other ways!   Over all brooded the stifling air.   ….Very soon indeed all the children were covered with the irritating rash of "prickly heat". That remains their clearest recollection of Calcutta to this day!   But it was not all unrelieved discomfort.   The lady in charge of the hostel did her best to make the refugees at home, sending in welcome cups of early tea, taking Muriel to the shops and showing many other kindnesses.

….Muriel lay awake night after night in the muggy darkness, struggling with her thoughts.   The rat ran merrily round the room….
Then she was offered a vacant bungalow in Shillong, the hill capital of Assam. She received help   from   sympathetic   friends.   However, the

journey to get there was to be long, complicated and dangerous. At one point kind hearted soldiers assisted her when she had to change trains. *...It was nine o'clock, pitch dark and raining hard when the train slowed to a stop in the junction. The troops were as good as their word. Some carried the children across the dripping, slippery platform, others saw to the baggage. Soon they were ensconced in their new compartment and awaiting the signal for departure*

......The night wore on, the party dozing fitfully. In the morning the train arrived at Amingaon, terminal station on the bank of the wide Brahmaputra River whence a ferry carries passengers across to Pandu and the train for Eastern Assam. From Pandu travellers to the latter hill-station continue their journey by car or bus along a road that climbs and twists for sixty-three miles into the heart of the Khasi Hills......On the steep hill road to Shillong one way traffic is strictly enforced, and rightly so, when one considers the narrowness of the road, its many dangerous turns and the precipices which border it. An unexpected swerve or a mechanical breakdown may send car and occupants plunging five hundred feet to the torrent below.

Muriel and her children reached the bungalow and were helped to settle in there by kind friends. At this time she could have had no idea what her husband was experiencing. Far away in the jungle and separated by ranges of high mountains his exhausted group had found a camp for the night after the day spent crossing the raging torrents of the Namyung Hka. Maggie the elephant, herself worn out, had helped some of the hundreds of others in the same plight. But there was to be no rest.

His account continues*: The crossing of the Patkai Range which now confronted us involved nearly sixty miles of hard travel and took us the next four days. We climbed to the 5000 ft. mark, almost a mile above sea-level, and down again in the course of a few hours. And all the road was mud. Rations were very short by now. A long day's march, on nothing more than two biscuits and a small piece of bully beef, is not the ideal form of hiking. It is not perhaps surprising that much of our conversation on the road dealt with food of various tempting kinds. The ideal breakfast, preferably eaten in bed with a pile of recent newspapers (we had had no news of the outside world for three weeks), a gourmet's dream of lunch, tea in the best teashop in Calcutta when if ever, we got there – these were some of the topics which helped to pass the long miles. Rushton craved for tinned pears; Crittle fancied masses of cream pastries; my idea of enjoyment was a mighty plate of sirloin. How greedy it all sounds! But anyone who has been on short commons in the* *jungle will sympathize, I feel sure.   And then when nearing the summit of some long climb, how alluring was the mental picture of a deep glass of fresh lime juice with ice tinkling at the brim!   Somehow lukewarm water from one's water-bottle never tasted quite as good!*

Though we travelled all day on May 24th, we failed to overtake the advance guard.   After her splendid exertions at the Namyung river, Maggie found the continual ascent very tiring, and her load heavier than ever.   Half-way up it was necessary to unload her and turn her loose for a graze and a rest.   At sunset therefore we were still far from a camp; earlier in the day we had passed one, rendered impossible by the presence of corpses, and pushed on.   Coming on a tiny stream of clear water that ran across the path half a mile below the crest, we stopped for the night in a big clump of bamboos.   The ground was deep in wet and rotting leaves, but what did that matter?   We made a shelter, we had fire and water.   In the middle of the night down came the rain to test out our leafy roof.   It was a good one, except in one spot where two halves joined.   As that faulty junction was immediately over my own bed, I had plenty of opportunity to study hydraulics: but at any rate it did enable me to fill my water-bottle!

The strain of the journey was beginning to tell on the health of the party.   Of two stragglers, Tidey, always utterly unselfish, with a companion, had gone back a mile or two down the hill and brough in one: the other had to stop the night in the bad camp we had passed and was fetched in next morning on a pony.

At this point Captain Gribble's story becomes slightly confused. He had said previously that he had agreed to go with the Padre, but now he seemed to be travelling with the Nagas under their guidance and benefitting from their knowledge of the jungle.

After spending another night in Tagap Ga he had been looking at his map of the high Ngalang ridge.   Ma Roi told him he would be the first white man to go to a remote village on the way, and that her sister who was married to the Duwa lived there.   *May 24th   I awakened very early and going down the 'ladder' I found G in heated argument with the muleteer, Lao Li, whom G had caught in the act of selling our tiny store of rice.   This was the last straw and Lao Li must have a lesson he would never forget.   I ordered the Nagas to tie his hands behind his back. Two guns were produced and carefully loaded and as the weapons were pointed at him I began to count ten.   He did not stay for the full count but bolted into the jungle taking the precious piece of rope   with   him.   We were not to see Lao Li again for many days but, before I was finished with him, there was to be one last encounter.*

About 8 a.m. I waved goodbye to Padre Crittle, and he, L and some others slopped through the mud into the gloom of the jungle. ...The Duwa and the old Akyiwa came to see me. The Duwa said, "Tomorrow I will take you to my village. The rain has started again and there is no hope of the refugees getting to the frontier. In fact, if we do not hurry it is doubtful whether we can cross the Tarung Hka. I have despatched some villagers to clear the track down the hillside and to get the raft repaired. If we start tomorrow morning we can arrive at my village the same day."...I told the Duwa we would set out early the next morning to his village....Then Ma Roi appeared from nowhere. "You will be the first white man to go to the Duwa's village," she said, "my sister is married to the Duwa and I have not seen her for a long time. I cannot now return to Shingbwiyang. We are frightened of the refugees and the horrors along the track. You are wise to consult the Duwa and other chiefs," she added. "No one will ever be able to live in this village again, the Duwa wants to burn it down."

The Duwa nodded and said, "We will not set fire to the village as long as any refugees remain here." "Good," I replied, "there is no hurry about appeasing the malignant spirits as they have done their damnedest already. The houses are useful as shelters to sick refugees."

All through the night I listened to groans and coughing of refugees, the rain and the fury of the wind. Our prospects for the morning were not bright. One thing was certain, I had stayed too long in this horrible place. I felt ill and when I lay down I was attacked with giddiness.

May 25th It would be tedious to stress the hardships of the journey today. For me they were particularly arduous because my feet were festering with a multitude of mud sores and it was as much as I could do to drag myself along avoiding the harder labours of the day.

Nothing could have excelled the thoughtfulness of the Duwa and others. All that morning we travelled on foot through the darkness of the forest, slowly descending a narrow and precipitous path which Sambaw said, "will bring us to the Kasi Hka" (cold water). We then follow that river to its junction with the Tarung Hka before we can cross to the opposite bank."

Under ordinary circumstances there would have been something alarming about that descent through the forest. Huge trees stood up like sentinels in every direction and entirely shut out the sunlight. The foliage was damp and as we slid step by step down the steep incline the villagers ahead of us could be heard chopping at branches and clearing a new path round fallen trees.

Ma Roi removed a huge leech from his leg. *..I was not alarmed however. On the contrary I was now feeling a sense of relief, soothed by the utter solitude which in that wilderness seemed to fall on the soul like a benediction. The horros of Tagap were behind us and the jungle now smelt sweet and was clean and peaceful.*

We descended the final slope to the Kasi Hka river to find the water rushing madly over the boulders. The Duwa who was in front of me stopped and said, "We shall have to follow this river to its junction with the Tarung Hka. There is a lot of water in it and we shall be delayed." They then led us into the watercourse and slowly we paddled through the water or stepped from boulder to boulder. Sometimes when the rush of water was fierce and deep, we clung to one another while, behind us, Topsy splashed and stumbled among the rocks as best as she could.

They camped during the afternoon....*The rain had ceased by this time. There were patches of blue and white overhead and the drone of aeroplanes could be heard quite plainly. Sometimes through the thick foliage I could see the outline of an aeroplane for a few seconds as it circled round....High green walls shut us in and except for a patch here and there, obscured the sky.*

Our shelter completed we settled down for the night among strange but cheerful companions, glad to be away from the shambles behind us. We all lay down in a row, the Duwa, the Akyiwa of the hoarse voice, seven Naga villagers and three Naga women, including Ma Roi. I was assured we would reach the Duwa's village the next afternoon. Then sleep took hold of me body and soul, and I knew nothing until wakened by Ray the next morning.

May 26th Gribble continued his journey with his companions. There seemed to be a network of Nagas helping them. They reached the Tarung Hka......*When I expressed doubts about being able to cross he (the Duwa) smiled and pointed to the opposite bank which was about 60 yards distant. "See," he said, "already the villagers are arriving to help us land on the other side. They will throw out long bamboo poles which the paddler will seize so that the raft, on nearing the other bank, can be safely secured at the landing place. As long as the landing-place is not under water it is safe to cross." I looked eagerly at the opposite bank and was cheered to see several figures, men and women, come* *bounding down the precipitous slope to the water's edge. It was also quite plain that, once safely across the rushing water, we were in for an incredibly stiff climb up the mountainside.*

He described the skill of the villagers in steering rafts across the fast flowing river. There is a sad story of how he went into the water with Topsy, his pony, and although he managed to swim to the bank with the help of a bamboo pole, she was swept away. *...I never expected to see Topsy again.*

There followed an exhausting steep climb to the village, and they arrived in sunlight. *...Other houses came in view, until I counted sixteen. Soon we were walking between them, watched by women, children and old men, peering from doorways or standing on the outside verandas. They looked a little scared or shy, but not unfriendly.....The climb to this Naga village had been far steeper than I had thought possible and yet those sturdy hill people showed little sign of fatigue, even though all of them had each carried a load that could not have been less than 100 lbs. in weight.*

During the night I was attacked by severe cramp in the legs. The muscles became knotted and painful. It was only after Ray had helped to massage my limbs and rub in ointment that I found it possible to sleep.

CHAPTER NINETEEN
May

'...But then before us we saw an absolute wall which seemed higher than anything we had so far encountered...' **Dr Russell**

Dr Russell's group were still on the refugee track and were suddenly given new hope by the presence of relief parties from Assam. *The sun shone brightly on Whit Monday, imparting almost a Bank-holiday feeling to the atmosphere as we ploughed through the mud to the valley-bottom. We entered a camp and there, to our astonishment and delight made our first contact with Assam. David Darlington, one of our missionaries who had gone through the hills with a survey party two months before was now working with the tea-planters who sought to succour the refugees coming from Burma. With two of these good fellows he had come as far as the little camp of Naungsum and there it was we met them 'Dr Livingstone, I presume!' almost seemed the correct greeting on so auspicious an occasion.*

Not only did they take their fellow-missionaries to their own little hut and regale us with Horlicks, they gave us fresh medical supplies and, more important still, information about the road that lay before us. A small bag of sago too was given to us, and provided a warm and filling meal that night. It was with considerably more cheerfulness that we turned again to the trail.

And truly we had need of cheerfulness. Our friends had told us that three ranges faced us that afternoon, each steeper than the last. The first two, though steep, were surmounted at last. But then before us we saw an absolute wall which seemed higher than anything we had so far encountered. As we laboured up the slippery path we hoped against hope that it would turn aside to some pass and miss the very summit. But, true to Naga custom, it climbed remorselessly to the very top, some 5000 ft. up, and there was nothing for us to do but the same. How glad we were at last to find the track turning downwards on the farther side!

A survey of the camp-site that evening revealed no level spot suitable for our party and sufficiently far from the crowded huts. Finally, after wading up a side stream for some distance we found a bank, dank and gloomy under the towering trees, where it was possible to clear a small space and erect a rough shelter. Across the stream our friends from Sahmaw followed our example. That night an unexpected treat was ours. One of their pack bullocks could go no further; at their request four of our party shot it and cut it up. The meat was divided, and a welcome addition it proved to our scanty rations. It was not far off midnight before a billy-can was passed to me. I lay back on my groundsheet, gnawing an exceedingly tough but tasty piece of beef! Next morning there was a bowl of hot soup for each man, and the chance to pick at a cold marrow-bone for those who liked such a treat.

As the last three or four of us climbed the hill through the camp on Tuesday morning, May 26th , we found an officer and a private lying in two little leaf shelters where they had been left sick by their party. We did what we could for them medically, and made sure they had supplies: there was a servant in attendance on them, and they were able to come on next day. (One of them, the private, I met subsequently in hospital in Shillong during August, and I was glad to learn that they both came through safely.)

Many were the topics we of the rearguard discussed on those long marches. Tidey, Crittle and I usually found ourselves together for many miles, though in the earlier stages Crittle was often busy with the pack ponies. He and Lazenby, one of our officers who had travelled widely in the remote regions of Asia Minor, nobly devoted themselves to the thankless task of loading and driving the two pack ponies the former had been able to buy at Tagap. Only those who have wrestled with the hide ropes by which loads are fastened to the pack saddle or tried to coax a refractory beast to carry the finished product can fully sympathize with the two men in their labours on our behalf.

After the morning's start conversation would flow fairly briskly from one to the other as we trudged along in single file. Then as the first fine free rapture of ploughing through the mud began to fade away, so would the conversation. For some time each busy with his thoughts, we were wont to carry on in silence. The second wind acquired, further topics would be bandied up and down the line. At last as the day wore on, tongues would cease to wag and each of us would find all his energies needed just to keep going, one foot after another, plodding along with only a dull wonder how much farther we should have to go that day.

The afternoon was wearing on when we reached the Tarung River and found a small ration camp on the farther bank. There two or three members of the Indian Tea-Planters' Association and a doctor were preparing to distribute rice and a little bullock-meat to the hungry crowd coming through. Some of us helped to drive them into some semblance of a queue: it needed the free exercise of one's lungs and not infrequently the use of a stout stick to gain the desired result. Many tried, not one nor twice, to slip into the head of the long line that was formed down one side of the muddy path, or to pass twice through the little shelter under which the food was distributed. Whilst we were thus engaged in the front, friend Tidey was to be seen armed with a large revolver and a tough expression, patrolling the rear of the enclosure to repel would-be looters. Undoubtedly the Church Militant was on the job!

A long string of stocky little Abor coolies came into the camp carrying heavy bags of rice. They wore little beyond a loin-cloth, a dah and an intriguing hat made of cane shaped very like a bowler, and so stoutly woven that it was proof against a lusty sword-cut – the Naga equivalent of the 'Battle bowler' of civilization.

Our delay at the camp meant that we could not hope to overtake the main body with the elephant before dark. Eight of us therefore camped in the valley bottom beside the rushing river with what little bedding and kit there was on the ponies. Never before or since had the sandflies been so numerous or so voracious as on that night. There was ample time for meditation as sleep was impossible for more than a few minutes at a time. It was a relief to get up and have a rest in the morning!

It was no fun on that long hill to be a sick man. Even for the fit it was hard work, and if one felt rotten and the strength had apparently gone from one's limbs, it was a nightmare. Two of our little party were far from well on Wednesday morning, May 27ᵗʰ, and had to take frequent turns on the one pony fit for riding. However sympathetic the rest of us may have felt, all we could do was to urge them on, for grim indeed was the prospect for any who fell by the wayside.

As we neared the crest the lowering clouds broke and a torrential rain added to our troubles. The track became a rushing stream of liquid mud. The trickling mountain brook was transformed into a raging torrent that burst into foam over the stepping stones, across which we picked an anxious passage, and went booming down into the valley below. Often from one's heart the almost inarticulate prayer 'O Lord, send some relief!' rose to the loving Father Who upholds in all circumstances, however adverse.

The rain ceased, but the grey evening did nothing to warm or dry soaked clothing. At a wayside ration hut hot tea, lacking milk or sugar but welcome nevertheless did much to brighten the picture. There, wisely, all travellers were disarmed: hereafter the teeth of would-be violence had been drawn and all men were equal.

The path lay through an evil swamp in which many a luckless pack animal foundered hopelessly and was rescued with difficulty. It was clear that the whole area would be rendered quite impassable by a day's rain. We picked our way through the mud and emerged upon the bank of a river. Silent and sinister it flowed, an oily swirl hinting at unplumbed depths. Round a corner it came into our view, and soon another curve in the valley hid it again. Tall trees stood somberly on the very edge of the dark water. No ray of sunshine lightened, no fresh breeze stirred the dank air. Like an unclean beast, the river seemed to be waiting to engulf unwary travellers.

Across this melancholy Styx travelled three flimsy bamboo rafts, their loud-voiced Charon a highly efficient Assamese sergeant of police. It was his task to prevent more than one or two passengers at a time with their bundles from essaying the crossing. All animals had to be swum over, and that was no easy task. The river was at least forty feet deep, the current very strong. It was not to be wondered at that the bullocks sometimes failed to reach the farther bank and were swept away into the gorge.

Whilst Tidey and I shouted and waved from the farther side others of our party led the ponies to the brink and then, catching them unawares, pushed them bodily over a four foot drop into deep water. Again and again the frightened animals swam out into the stream, and half-way across: then, turning aside they would seek the shelter of the trees from which they had come. At last, a gallant member of the Sahmaw party, Roland, who had pressed on in spite of a badly scalded foot, stripped, plunged into the water and swam across, the bridle of his pony in his hand. The others followed, and one after the other, blowing and panting, were dragged up on to the bank. One of the Sahmaw bullocks was lost, but that was our only tribute to the evil genius of the place!

Three more miles in the fading light whilst our wet clothes dried on our backs brought us to Shamlang, a small ration camp deep in the jungle. An hospitable planter issued most welcome tinned stores to us, and our worthy cook prepared a mighty stew over the cheerful camp fire. For the night's lodging we had part of a large hut, in which a number of sick and exhausted Indians lay, muffled like mummies in their blankets. Our luxurious mattress consisted of parallel wooden poles, across which we turned from side to side, truly thankful that we each possessed two sides on which to lie in turn. But at any rate the roof over our heads was waterproof, and that after all is the most important part of any shelter.

CHAPTER TWENTY
May

'...I felt a creepy sensation down my spine but I did not continue the subject just then. I knew that if the Duwa and his villagers decided not to come with us to the frontier, we should be in a sorrier plight than ever...' **Captain Gribble**

Now in a very remote Naga village away from the well worn track, Captain Gribble was having a break from the oppressive damp of the jungle. He and Ray could bathe in clear water and enjoy a moment in the sunshine.

May 27th It was a sunny morning with a crispness in the air that was remarkable for the time of year and the view of the rough, wooded, broken, precipitous hills was now fully exposed. The 'river of death' was hidden in the valley below but, across the intervening space to the opposite ridge, the villages of Tagap Ga were just visible.

Ray and I found a crystal clear spring spurting from the mountain side, and discarding our muddy clothes we bathed in the glistening water. Afterwards we sat on the grass warming our exhausted bodies in the sunlight. The view of the forest clad hills around us was grand and it was difficult to imagine the horrible tragedy unfolding itself in the silence of those wooded sunlit hills.

However their feet and ankles were covered in sores, their personal possessions were very few. *...Our own scanty store of food would enable us to partake of two tiny meals a day for about six or seven days, consisting of rice and a little curry-washed down with 'Kachin' tea without milk or sugar, and it was evident that we must, for our own safety, meet the local chiefs without delay...*

To his great joy and relief his pony had been found and brought back. He was amazed that she had survived the rapids. *....As the sun was setting I sat on a log in an old clearing about one mile from the village, and surveyed the wild mountainous country that extended to the far horizon. In our parlous condition the prospect of surmounting those precipitous ranges looked horribly formidable. Fold after fold of wooded hills in every direction; the ridges to the North looked particularly forbidding.*

"The trail to the Assam frontier lies in that direction," said the Duwa, pointing to the north. " The high range in the distance is called the 'Nga-lang Bum'. "Where is the Assam boundary?" I asked. "We cannot see it," he replied, "it lies behind the Nga-lang Bum, and is seven days' march from here. I am scared about proceeding further during the rains. I may not be able to recross the rivers and, moreover, I hear

that numerous people have died on the trek and their sprawling bodies would be close companions for us all day and every day."

I felt a creepy sensation down my spine but I did not continue the subject just then. I knew that if the Duwa and his villagers decided not to come with us to the frontier, we should be in a sorrier plight than ever.

As they gazed across the valley Gribble saw planes near Tagap Ga. *...The Duwa, without any show of excitement, told me that at the time Topsy arrived a villager had brought in the news that a rope had been dropped by an aeroplane at Lower Tagap and crowds of refugees had successfully crossed the river and were hastening along the track towards the frontier.* On hearing this Gribble reflected that the grim situation would be somewhat eased.

This was news indeed! For some days the weather had undergone a remarkable providential change for the better, and if the rain held off a few days longer the situation at Tagap would be transformed. Thousands of refugees, now held up, would be able to push on to the frontier and the hopeless alternative of trying to form a Refugee Colony would not need further thought. Moreover, we too could take advantage of the weather, and perhaps reach the frontier before the rains started again.

The Duwa said the other chiefs were expected tomorrow and I decided to wait another day in order to meet them In any case we were sorely in need of more rest.

Dr Russell's group had spent the night in a hut in Shamlang where there was again help from the Tea-planters, with the promise of more regular camps along the way. The journey itself was very difficult and dangerous, making their way up and down steep slippery mountain tracks. *..The early morning brought wailing and a good deal of teeth-gnashing, figuratively at any rate, amongst our friends of the Sahmaw party. Some bold opportunist had seized his chance and stolen a bag which contained, besides a large sum of money, all the vital papers of the Company which had been carried carefully two hundred miles to Shamlang. In spite of search they were not recovered, as far as I know.*

In the past, one had felt very little sympathy with the young man of Longfellow's famous poem who, if we may interpret the familiar words in the speech of today, had gone beetling up the pass, waving his little banner until he got what was coming to him, and was properly browned off in a snowdrift. But even if any old man had advised us to 'Try not the pass!' it is certain we should not have listened that Thursday morning, May 28th. As they told us before we left the camp at Shamlang, the

MAY

Pangsau Pass, dividing line between India and Burma, was only about three miles in front of us. Once over it we should find regular system of ration camps, waterproof shelters for the night, and other evidences of advanced civilization. No! We were all in favour of 'Excelsior' and his mountain-climbing efforts!

The actual Pass however was remarkably dull. After rising steadily for an hour or so we found the path began to descend, at first uncertainly, as if not quite sure of its own mind, but then more definitely. We realized we were indeed out of Burma and into Assam. There were no notices in a foreign language, no officious Customs people. The mud was just as glutinous, the jungle smelt the same, the hawk-billed cuckoo still uttered its monotonous cry that sounded like 'Lazy people, lazy people!' But we were out!

Soon we reached a deserted Naga village perched on a steep hill-side, the verandas of the huts projecting like the bows of a ship out over the drop below. The clouds had been gathering and a fine rain began to fall. It was obvious that, however pleasant a short rest might have been it was advisable to push on with all speed. The steep path would rapidly become very slippery when wet. For nearly a mile the side of the hill had been cleared for cultivation; the path was beaten hard, and soon resembled a skating rink. It was a relief to plunge into the jungle again and find, to our surprise, a small shelter under which boiled two big cauldrons of tea for the refreshment of weary pilgrims.

As we seem to have 'gone all literary' in this chapter, a further quotation seems apposite here. In Bunyan's immortal allegory, Christian is reported as saying: 'As it was difficult coming up, so, so far as I can see, it is dangerous going down.' 'Yes,' said Prudence, 'so it is; for it is a hard matter for a man to go down into the Valley of Humiliation as thou art now, and to catch no slip by the way,' So he began to go down the hill, but very warily; yet he caught a slip or two.'

We too went very warily down the long slopes that still lay before us as the rain sheeted down and the mud sucked the shoes from our feet. But I, at any rate, caught half a dozen slips, as my feet went from under me. It was more like skiing in places: one launched oneself down the path, hoping to keep one's balance; but sometimes one was unlucky! It would have been easy to break an ankle against a hidden stone or projecting root, but throughout all the journey, our feet were graciously kept.

The march seemed long enough that day, but when we reached Nampong, the first of the string of Rest-camps organized by the Indian

Tea-Planters Association, we found it was apparently shorter than we had thought. Owing to the difference between Burma Summer time, and Indian Standard Time, we had to put our watches back two hours. In future the sun rose at four a.m. and set at six p.m. It took several days to get used to the change in the timing of the day.

There was a stream to be crossed before we entered the camp, the sight of which from the hill had spurred our flagging footsteps. But there was no need for us to wade, though our shoes could not have been made any wetter than they were. A fine suspension bridge spanned the stream, the forerunner of others to come. There were to be no more flimsy rafts or precarious stepping-stones for us.

(sfr)

MAY

Outside a hospital hut a dresser waited to attend to sore feet, a Canadian doctor examined more serious cases. We were directed to shelters, roofed with thatch and tarpaulin, where we could spend the night. At hand was a booth in which rich dhall (lentils) and onions were already cooked, merely needing the sauce of a ravenous appetite. Never has any seven-course dinner at a luxury hotel tasted as good as a lavish helping of those humble ingredients, eaten from a dirty mess-tin, and washed down with copious draughts of hot tea. Then, more wonderful still there followed an issue of biscuits and cheese! How long was it since we had tasted cheese! A matter of weeks! Henceforth, we were never to be out of reach of food or shelter. A proper rest-camp was situated about every ten miles, with lesser tea-camps at shorter intervals.

That last long hill had proved too much for one of our party and Bruce, one of our officers, failed to come in. A brother officer, Rae, the young giant who had so splendidly cared for two riding ponies was with him; and others coming in said the sick man was on a stretcher and being carried down to the camp. We anxiously awaited his arrival but darkness fell and still he had not reached the camp. In the morning Crittle and I addressed ourselves to the hill again, and after a gruelling ascent found the sick man and his companion where they had been left by their cooolies at night-fall. Fortunately the night was dry and fairly warm and they had a blanket: but such treatment is not the best for serious illness. They eagerly sampled the flask of tea, biscuits and bully beef we had brought up with us. Then, with the help of a planter we were able to enlist twelve stocky little Abor coolies to carry the stretcher down to Nampong. Barefooted and hardly burdened with clothing though they were, it was a remarkable performance they put up. On muddy slopes where we had difficulty in standing they ran with the stretcher carried shoulder-high. They scampered down the hill leaving us mere pedestrians far in the rear.

At Nampong it was necessary to surrender all our animal transport to the planters, as it was realized that their hooves would cut up the track too badly and jeopardize the successful carrying up of supplies by the long strings of coolies on whom the camps depended. Maggie had faithfully brought us this far: hereafter we found it was possible to hire the coolies as they returned empty to carry our bundles. It was arranged the the elephant should be handed over to the authorities for the evacuee work. The next morning when the mahout went out to look for Maggie he found only the end of a broken chain; though he trailed her right up the hill, he did not succeed in catching her again. She had gone. Thus at Shingbwiyang God provided her to meet our need: at Nampong, her work was finished and He took her away.

'…he is welcome to anything we have, including my spare socks, but not my scalp…' **Captain Gribble**

Captain Gribble had spent some time in the remote Naga village where he was possibly the first white man to be seen. He was feeling anxious and threatened by unfamiliar faces. *May 28th We sat round the hearth in the Duwa's house discussing events with the Chief of Wurang, and other who had arrived that morning. He was darker than the usual Naga with black piercing beady eyes. "I returned from the frontier a few days ago with my villagers," he said, "they have been helping to clear the track. Now the rains have come we can do no more and are hastening back to our villages."*
"What chance have the refugees of reaching the frontier? I asked. "The refugees must go on if it is humanly possible," he replied, pulling out a white metal box from his bag and opening it to take a pinch of tobacco. "Look," whispered Dr Ray to me in English, "it is a medical syringe box." I nodded and winked.
…"If you go on," said the Chief, looking at me with his beady eyes, "you too will have to abandon all you possess before you get over the ridge." "That won't be much," I said to Ray in English, "he is welcome to anything we have, including my spare socks, but not my scalp." I looked at this Chief with renewed interest for there was something about him that made me feel uncomfortable. Could he be a head-hunter?
I was not aware that the Nagas in these, the eastern range of the Naga Hills, practiced head-hunting any longer, but in the present confused circumstances anything might happen. Only that morning I had seen a skull, fixed to the end of a bamboo pole, carefully hoisted and planted in front of one of the houses in the village…. To my relief the Chief of Wurang announced his intention of leaving the next morning for his village which could be seen situated high up on the slope of a far off ridge. "My villagers have done a lot of work and are tired. We must reach our village before the rains set in again," he said. I was glad he was going for it was clear he would not help either the refugees or ourselves and, furthermore, I did not feel the confidence in him that I felt in the Duwa. Tomorrow we would make our way back to Tagap and if possible push on to the Namyng river crossing.
May 29th But the next day they did not leave yet as Gribble felt feverish and Ray advised him to rest for another day. Topsy regained some strength grazing below the village where there was plenty of grass.

They enjoyed more hospitality from the Nagas. Ma Roi appeared with bags of clothes, sheets, towels and dress material of many colours which she had found discarded at Tagap Ga "...*I shall choose some clothing for myself, and the rest will be distributed among the women in the village. Each sheet, torn in half, will make two suitable raiment for a woman, and will save the trouble of having to weave a garment in the village. The cotton crop was bad this year," she added slyly. "As you see, most of the females only wear a single piece of material tucked in at the breast and worn short to the knees.*

By this time the Duwa's house was crowded with women and children. After selecting some of the more colourful material for herself, Ma Roi distributed the rest among her friends. There was much laughter and rejoicing. Later on I received many small gifts of rice and Indian corn brought to me on platters by the women. My feelings were strangely mixed by these undeserved gestures of appreciation.

About sunset Ray and I strolled across to the house occupied by Ma Roi and her married sister. As we climbed the steps leading into the house there was the sound of talk, of laughter, and the air was tainted with the smoke of fires filtering up through the thatch of the house like dedicated incense into the hollow firmament above.

We were received by the smiling owner of the house. He was a lean, middle aged man, clad in a loin cloth, his brown shining body looked exceedingly muscular. We were made to sit on the little wooden stools near the hearth in the guests' apartment while the house owner set about brewing some tea. I glanced round the room and noticed that the walls, as in the Duwa's house, were hung with the trophies of the chase. There were horns and skulls in profusion.

After distributing the tea in little wooden bowls our host prepared an opium pipe for himself. When all were comfortable he told us of the spirits that guarded the village and about the Duwa who had persuaded him to leave Tagap ten years ago and help establish this village in a more healthy climate. "Tagap village which you have just left," he said, "belongs to another world called Mithi-kwa (dead-man's village). The Duwa was wise to bring us away from there. He must have foreseen the tragedy.

Changing the subject he said, "Ma Roi's father is a big chief and lives at the foot of those hills, " pointing vaguely to the west. "I had to pay numerous hpagas (gifts) in order to marry her sister. She is a good woman and has borne me three children...

...Ma Roi was as well informed as ever. She said, "The Duwa told me

you will return to the Tagap ridge tomorrow and that he will accompany you together with some of the villagers. They will go with you as far as Namlip, three marches from here, but cannot go further for fear of being cut off by the river. This fine weather cannot last much longer," she added, "you would be wise to stay here until the end of the rainy season. "What a terrible prospect that would be," I thought, "no books, no paper to write on and apart from the terrible food difficulties, no clothing or companionship. It is plain we must face the horrors of that jungle track, in the hope that we shall win through to safety."

Wilfred Crittle wrote: *...For some days Bruce had not been at all well – suffering from a severe cold and what seemed to be malaria. (It was later diagnosed as pneumonia) He had been riding one of the ponies for the last two days and we had passed him and Captain Rae who was walking with him some miles up the road. When they did not come by evening we began to feel anxious. Just about dark an officer appeared riding the pony. He told us that Bruce had become too ill to ride a horse. So he had handed over his stretcher and coolies to him and taken his pony, for as his was only a leg injury he could ride quite well. Russell and I sat on the river bank till 10.30 before going to bed but there was no sign of the stragglers.*

Next morning after a meal we thought we had better go and see what had happened, so Russell and I set off with food, water and medicines and retraced our steps up the hill. Some three miles up we came across Bruce on his stretcher with Rae sitting alongside. They had spent the night there, the coolies having gone on strike and fled. We had fortunately just seen a planter going up to one of the other camps and he kindly lent us some coolies who carried Bruce into camp...'

Lieutenant Bruce being carried on a stretcher   (sfr)

Dr Russell described the moment when Bruce was accidentally tipped off his stretcher. All sick refugees were very vulnerable once they were unable to walk. When this happened '... *We were some miles from Nampong which we had left long after the main party had gone on. It was necessary to wait for the coolies who were to carry the invalid on for the next stage, until the middle of the morning of Saturday, May 30th. So far ahead did the others get that the half-dozen forming the rearguard did not overtake them until the end of the journey at Margherita, four days later. Before we left the camp where we had met with so much kindness, one of the officials actually handed us a typewritten bulletin of the wireless news after a month of being cut off from the great world outside.*

No praise is too high for the labour of those tea-planters who volunteered for the work of succouring the helpless refugees from Burma. Running isolated camps in the jungle, organizing coolie-transport for the supply of food, or the carrying of the many sick, searching out and bringing in those who fell by the way, they undoubtedly saved many lives and earned our undying gratitude. Tea-planters' hospitality must be experienced to be understood. The letters 'I.T.A.' (Indian Tea-Planters' Association) stood in our minds as a splendid answer to three others, 'S.O.S.'

Another downpour made the going so heavy that the four coolies had great difficulty in standing let alone carrying a heavy stretcher. In places the path was only a foot wide, and we watched anxiously as they crawled past the bad patches. It took us four hours to do three miles and exhausting travel we found it. It was therefore with great relief that we reached a little intermediate camp, Namgoi, where the Englishman in charge invited us to stay the night. His hospitality was lavish indeed. Tea, actually with milk and sugar, a new tarpaulin to spread over the floor of our hut, a dish of boiled potatoes for supper, tinned fruit and soup for the invalid, a hurricane lamp instead of a feeble candle – there was no limit to his kindness. It was a greatly refreshed party that set out to the next camp at Namchik on Sunday morning, May 31st.

Captain Gribble was heading back towards the refugee trail. *May 30th By 1 p.m. we had descended the mountain side and were once again on the right bank of the Tarung Hka waiting for the villagers to cross....After a short halt we turned our backs on the Tarung Hka and pushed our way through the jungle to the Kasi Hka, and it was soon evident that we would not reach the Tagap ridge that night.*

MAY/JUNE

The Kasi tributary had more water in it than we liked to see, and we had to pick our way from side to side jumping from boulder to boulder, sometimes leaving the river bed where the water was too deep and cutting our way through the jungle to point further up the river.

About 5 p.m. we decided to halt....it was a thoroughly miserable night, and the insects added to our discomfort. I tried to sleep but was disturbed by the thought that the river might rise suddenly and wash us away.

May 31st They made their way through the stream and then climbed the steep slope towards Tagap village. The Nagas guided the group along various tracks. *...By noon the mist had cleared, and on the path in front of us was a bamboo stockade surrounding a large field containing a crop of millet. "The stockade," said Sambaw, "is to prevent bands of refugee looters from stealing our crops. We are now within one mile of the track leading to the Namyung Hka from Tagap."...As soon as we opened a gap in the stockade the little party of severn Naga men and two women, Sambaw, Ray and myself passed through and shortly after reached the track that led down the ridge to the Namyung Hka. The Nagas bore off to the right and joined the stream of refugees heading for the river. I followed them, plodding along the mud-laden track as best as I could. I noticed that the air was heavy with a sickening stench, the most awful of all smells that man can be called to endure, because it preyed on the imagination as well as the senses ...I felt that others like these were to be our close companions all day and beyond on succeeding days....*

...The track ankle deep in mud, was a series of precipitous climbs and descents. Presently with the noise of water in our ears, we realized we were not far from the place where, in recent days, so many people had lost their lives trying to cross the turbulent waters of the Namyung Hka......

...Lost in the green hell of a jungle with little or no food, the fear of death at every turn and not knowing how far they had yet to travel before reaching civilization again, those that could endure hurried on and the weaker fell by the wayside. And yet those who continued long enough, provided their strength remained, hoped they would find their way through the open window, to safety.

The crossing at the Namyung Hka was about 150 yards wide. The temper of the river was fierce, and the water tumbled and bellowed over the boulders in an alarming manner....The water was from 4' to 5' deep and it was difficult to keep one's feet. Without the rope-way it would have been extremely dangerous or impossible to cross.

Gribble and Ray crossed successfully and Ma Roi appeared on the opposite bank and swam across. ....*Ma Roi said,"I travelled fast to catch you up. There are no more villages along the route until you pass the frontier which is many difficult marches from here. I am going to see my relatives living among the Warung Ni on the hills overlooking the Namlip valley. The Duwa's villagers will not go any farther than that place but he will try and get some of the Warung villagers to help you. You must hurry while the weather remains fine.*" Sambaw advised them to proceed along the edge of the river and they later sheltered for the night on a clean sandy beach surrounded by a huge tree and bamboos.

June 1st Last night was as black as pitch – no moon, no stars – only the slight patter of rain on the leaves..... Topsy the pony was stolen in the night and Gribble and Ray had to walk for an hour the following day to claim her back from a stranger...*We...set out at once to rejoin the Nagas who were waiting for us on the track leading to Namlip...I learned that the bulk of the people, held up for over a week at Tagap, had since the remarkable break in the monsoon successfully crossed the river and gone on hurriedly towards the frontier. Others, perhaps a thousand a day were still passing, but their numbers were dropping daily. "The Japs,"* said one Indian, *"have reduced Mandalay to ashes, and their bombers are operating all over the country. They are a barbarous foe and have butchered many of their prisoners."*

By evening they reached an encampment...*When Sambaw arrived he said, "The river water is polluted, we cannot camp here." He led the way up the track and presently plunged into the jungle to a shelf of land near a tiny stream."*

Gribble was aware of their urgent need to persuade other porters to help them. *"Tomorrow," I said to Ray, "we shall halt here. Our few porters are afraid to go any farther. There is a village on the top of the mountain nearby. I shall go up there in the morning and ask the local chief to help us."*

June 2nd I could not but admire the physical shapeliness of the Nagas. With their supple limbs and strong features they suggested in each graceful movement of their bodies immense strength and stamina. With leaders the like of Sambaw they were capable of becoming great warriors in the art of jungle warfare. If properly trained the Japanese would find them a tough nut to crack. At odd times for several days I heard sudden short bursts of machine gun fire. The sound of firing was *always ahead of us and I concluded that there were parties in front trying to keep up their spirits by firing aimlessly into the jungle. Tomorrow we could perhaps catch up with some of them. Our next march would be an all day climb over the Ngalang ridge (4900 feet)*

Gribble and Ray were now back on the refugee track which was in a bad state. ....*My map shows the country ahead to be extremely rough and precipitous, forever engulfed in a forest so thick that the sun's rays cannot penetrate. For many days to come we would have to tramp from dawn to dusk along a malaria infested jungle track laden with mud, and with the prospect of numerous formidable rivers to cross. We dare not ask ourselves if we could do it but encouraged ourselves, as we encouraged others along the way.*

With Sambaw he visited a village where a network of porters were persuaded to assist him the following day, taking over from Sambaw's porters who were anxious to return to their villages. ...*At about 7 a.m. the Duwa and I, together with a strange Naga villager whose face I had not seen before set out to find a village situated on a ridge overlooking the Namlip Valley....We climbed over 2000 feet before reaching the village. Here we entered a small bamboo hut supported on stilts and found an old Naga man inside. While Sambaw explained things to him, I went outside and sat in the sun.*

The view was magnificent and ridge after ridge of broken hills stood out in all directions. Sambaw came out of the hut and stood beside me. "Tomorrow we have to climb that hill and the ridge beyond it," he said "and it will take us all day." Gribble was given a freshly cooked meal by the Nagas before climbing down the valley again with Sambaw.

CHAPTER TWENTY TWO
June

'...This young daughter of a Naga chief would be long remembered for her intelligence and cheerfulness...' **Captain Gribble**

The time had come for Captain Gribble to leave Ma Roi behind. He too was soon to meet relief workers from Assam. But later his journey was to go in an entirely different direction.

June 3rd Soon after dawn a few villagers arrived at our shelter and took over the loads from Sambaw's porters, anxious to return to their village as they had brought only a limited quantity of food.   These were the days of starvation and it was becoming more difficult from day to day to check our hunger from becoming tyrannous, and to prevent our weariness from getting us down.   Ma Roi was looking a little crestfallen as she watched us depart.   She said she would stay in the village on the mountain until Sambaw returned from the frontier and then go back with him by a shorter but more difficult path.   This young daughter of a Naga chief would be long remembered for her intelligence and cheerfulness.

The way they followed was strewn with corpses....we were experiencing a feeling of horror at the tragedies around us, but suddenly our horror gave way to astonishment for I saw approaching us down the slope of the hill – two Europeans with a party of porters behind them. With a strange feeling of relief I hastened to meet them.

They were members of an advanced party sent out from Assam to form a relief camp in the Ngalang jungle.   After greetings and a short discussion, they decided to halt for the night and go on the next morning into the Namlip valley where many refugees were in a state of exhaustion and could not face the climb to the top of Ngalang Bum without food and first aid.

As several hours of daylight still remained, Ray and I resumed our journey to the top of the mountain (4900 ft).   We arrived at the summit in time to help collect and distribute bags of food dropped by aircraft on a bare patch of ground. ...We had marches all today, and the sun had set before we found a camping place for the night.   The sides of the track were littered with clothing and other personal belongings that had been cast away as the steep prolonged ascent to the mountain top brought exhaustion to toiling ant-like humanity. The jungle was so thick that we did not trouble to erect a shelter. Wrapping ourselves in blankets we turned in for the night.

They slept briefly but then were disturbed when it seemed as though some large animal was nearby…*My pony was tethered near me and I could hear her crunching leaves. She stopped crunching. I sat up and let out a yell. There was immediately a crashing of branches and crackling of leaves as something heavy fled deeper into the jungle. It was gone.*

I felt cold, miserable and itching from bites. The whisper and droning of the forest was horribly disturbing. "In a few hours we will be gone from this place," I said to myself, "Night will soon be gone." I put out my hand and felt Ray near me. After this I must have fallen asleep and only awoke when the tree tops were burnished with colour.

Dr Russell had been refreshed at a Tea planters' camp at Namgoi. *The stage was a mere eight or nine miles, but the constant hindrance of the ever-present mud made it enough. My shoes were bound with webbing tape, cut from my little daughter's bedstead before I left Mohnyin: that alone kept the soles from parting company altogether with the uppers.*

The chief feature of Monday's march was one that we could well have done without. Owing to some little mistake on the part of the camp cook the night before each was afflicted with 'fightings and fears within' which necessitated frequent sudden departures for the jungle along the road. As in many places the path was bordered by a sheer bank on one hand, and an equally sheer drop on the other, that day's march was not one of the most carefree of the whole trip! We need say no more!

Up and up went the track, climbing at last to the hill-top camp of Kumlao. It was the last big ascent of the whole long journey though we did not realize it at the time. From our shelter for the night we looked out across far distances to the steaming plains of Assam, hazy and inviting in the setting sun. From that jungle panorama we gazed into the land of promise, for which we had longed so earnestly, and towards which we had travelled so far.

In the months since December the Japanese had rapidly occupied almost all of Burma and halted around this time because the monsoon. They had reached the Chindwin River and were just south of the Indian frontier in the west.

Although aided by the regular relief camps along the way, Dr Russell's struggle to keep going was not yet over. *Came the dawn of our last day of journey, Tuesday June 2nd. The sun peeped over the crest of the hill, sending long shadows across the plain below and covering the dew-soaked foliage with diamonds. The air was cool and refreshing as* we set out down the hill, from time to time meeting a line of coolies carrying up supplies to the camps, or a train of sturdy pack-mules. After some miles we reached the top of the 'Golden Stair' where the path dropped hundreds of feet in a flight of rough steps, made by putting branches across the muddy path. The sight of several abandoned stretchers lying by the roadside at the top gave a significant hint, and we sat on the bank just round the corner until the litter arrived on which lay one of the party. As we suspected, the coolies, reluctant to face the trouble of carrying a sick man down that fearsome staircase, put it down and began to lift him off, telling him that the camp was only just at the bottom and he had better walk. As we found later, there lay before us one of the worst two miles of all. When Crittle, Tidey and I appeared round the corner, however, nonchalantly waving our stout sticks and saying 'Go on!' they suffered a sudden change of mind, picked up the stretcher again and addressed themselves to the descent. There was no further trouble until we reached camp! It is difficult to believe, but in at least one instance a sick man was tipped off into the jungle by his coolies and left to die.

So bad was the mud in the valley-bottom as the track wound along the bank of the river that it was not infrequent after rain for weary travellers to be so hopelessly stuck that rescue parties were needed to find them and pull them out. We could well believe it, and were truly thankful that there had been no rain for a day or two. As it was, we were sufficiently weary when we reached the big camp at South Tirap to enjoy an hour's rest, and more of that life-giving tea. The hollow feeling behind our belts too helped to remind us that we had not breakfasted yet, though it was midday; biscuits did something to assuage the pangs, but not enough...

... We crossed the long suspension bridge slung from giant trees and embarked upon the last stage. The road broadened out, cut from the red earth of the hill-side, and it was possible to walk three abreast. Before us moved a procession of stretchers, sick being carried to the next camp. As we gazed down upon them from a higher level small figures silhouetted against the steep red banks, we were reminded of pictures of the funeral procession of some ancient Egyptian Pharaoh being carried to his rock-hewn tomb in the hills of Thebes.

Across the valley rose the hills, and it was sweet to realize that we at least had no need to climb them; they were behind us, and the road still led downhill. Then without warning it happened!! At 3.23 p.m. coming down a long slope, we all heard the hoot of a train! The last time we had heard that most musical sound had been a month before, and three *hundred miles away. Can it be wondered that we burst into the strains of 'Glory, glory Alleluia' as we went marching down, our weariness forgotten?*

(sfr)

A brief rest to drink more tea and write our names in a register of evacuees, and we made our way to railhead where two Diesel cars awaited us. They rapidly filled up with refugees, Indian and English. Our faithful staves were cast from the door, now no longer needed, bundles were piled upon the floor. As the cars began to move there appeared upon every face the same rather foolish smile. The landscape was going past and we were not doing it!

The cars stopped and we had to change into the long refugee train that stood with steam up waiting to go. There was other accommodation available, but we preferred to pile into an empty coal-wagon in which our stretcher-borne friend could lie flat. Slowly the train clanked over the points and gathered speed. With one voice, sick and healthy alike we joined in the words of the familiar hymn, 'Now thank we all our God, with hearts and hands and voices!' And truly it came from each heart in the grimy wagon.

Margherita station. Long fences of barbed wire. The rest of our party awaiting us in the rest camp. Formalities at the entrance, registration slips to be filled up. The name of our fathers, our permanent addresses, (if we had any!), our destinations. At last, as darkness fell the smooth grass of the golf-course on which the tents were pitched.

They, the camp authorities made us welcome, issued to each man a new pair of shorts, shoes, socks, a grey shirt, loaned us bedding for the night. Then, wonderful to relate, a pail of hot water and the first hot bath for a month! No wonder we all felt it was a beautiful dream as we gathered in the mess marquees to eat off china plates, to drink out of china cups, to sit on chairs with backs!

Crittle and I shared a tent. After so long on the ground or on bamboo poles a camp bed seemed too good to be true. We commended ourselves once again into the keeping of our gracious God Who has led us so wonderfully and so far; blew out the lamp and sank into a heavy sleep.

Of course it was too good to be true! In the middle of the night an uneasy dream became reality and I awakened to the growl of thunder and the approaching patter of rain. Then the storm burst upon the camp. The tent rocked and flapped whilst Crittle and I hung on to the poles. The rain poured down and drove across the tent floor. From the safety of our beds we looked down into a pool inches deep, which threatened to submerge our nice dry shoes and socks. No! Come what might we would not, could not, face wet socks again! We rescued them and piled as many of our possessions as we could upon our camp beds. Then, like St Paul, we 'cast four anchors out of the stern and wished for the day'.

The day came in, grey and depressing, but what was a little water to hardened travellers like ourselves? After breakfast we made enquiries as to our future movements. Letters were waiting for Crittle and Rushton, but never a word from my wife – she had written but none of her letters reached me till much later. Where she was in the whole wide land of India I had not the faintest idea. It was possible that she and the little ones had gone South, down to Kodaikanal perhaps. The only thing was to go to Calcutta and there try to pick up the trail. Everyone agreed that it was a waste of time to send telegrams so great was the congestion on the wires. Faithlessly I must admit the thought came to me, perhaps there was bad news of the family, and Crittle or Rushton had been asked to break it gently! But such fears were soon banished.

Before our train left at 5 p.m. there was much to do. Some of our party had been lodged in hospital for the night and we had them to visit. Our Burmese money had to be changed into Indian currency at the golf hut around which milled a clamouring crowd of Indians all brandishing their notes. In the middle of the group one unluckly coolie burst into tears finding his poor savings had just been filched from him by some scoundrel. There was the doctor to be seen lest we bring some infectious disease into India. Food, too, for the long railway journey must be procured, more tea drunk and goodbyes said. The military members of our little band were to leave next morning, so it was at Margherita that our party finally broke up. Splendid fellows, may God bless them and bring them safely back to their distant homes!

Dr Russell and his friends continued on their long journey. *Crittle, Rushton, Pearson and I left by train that night en route for Calcutta. All that night and all the next day we rumbled across Assam. There was nothing to read, nothing to be bought at a wayside station. From time to time we talked, slept, gazed at the monotonous landscape or dipped into our tinned provisions. At last late at night we reached Pandu on the banks of the wide Brahmaputra but only to find that the last ferry had gone hours before, and there was no crossing before next morning.*

It seemed a set-back, but it was all part of the plan. The hard boards of the ferry flat were our beds that night. In the early morning the ferry boat moved over to us, cutting a long furrow in the still river. We carried our ragged bundles on to the deck. To our disappointment there was no food available. We leaned against the railing awaiting the signal for departure.

Just before the time for crossing a fellow-passenger who had come on board a few minutes earlier got into conversation with Crittle. Suddenly the latter called across to me: 'Our friend here says your wife is in Shillong!' It transpired that the newcomer, a chaplain from Dibrugarh had actually been host to Mrs Crittle when she and my wife had been flown out from Myitkyina in April. He had seen a photograph of Crittle and recognized him from it. And more important still to me at least, he believed my family were at that moment in Shillong, only seventy miles away! There was no time to lose and a friendly officer gave me the use of his telephone.   A call to the Chaplain of Shillong, even so early was promptly put through, and he gladly confirmed the news of my wife's whereabouts.

Hurriedly I carried my baggage off the ferry and watched it leave on its way over to the far bank, whilst I waited for a car to carry me on the last stage of my wanderings;   for all unknowing, I had come by the shortest route to Shillong.   I had time, once again, to ponder the Lord's wonderful dealings with me.

Little more need be said.   Before mid-day my car entered Shillong, 5000 ft above the heat of the plains.   As I collected my things from the back another car drove up.   The tall figure of our kind friend the Chaplain advanced towards me, his hand out-stretched in greeting. Behind him I saw the face of my dear wife. My journey was over at last!

CHAPTER TWENTY THREE
June

'…we were soon to regret we ever left the mud trail for a journey that nearly brought us to complete destruction….' **Captain Gribble**

Captain Gribble was now back on the refugee track with a new group of Naga porters. *June 4th There was a strange absence of birds in this desolate jungle. Occasionally one did catch a glimpse of a dark feathered bird about the size of a butcher bird. Their cries as they flew sounded as though each bird was calling us to "go it". "The bird is a wise one," said Ray, "we will go it fast enough."*

They arrived at a relief camp. Though they did not know it there were still great dangers ahead. *…There were three Europeans in the camp, a doctor and two tea planters. They had volunteered in answer to the call made by the Authorities to the Indian Tea Association. Only sick refugees were detained in the camp. All others were given food and encouraged to push on to the frontier….Presently the Camp Commandant brought along a prisoner. It was Lao Li, the muleteer! "I arrested him for hanging about the camp and for insolence," said the officer-in-charge. "The prisoner admits that he knows you." "He certainly does," I replied, "he deserted at Tagap Ga after stealing rice. I will deal with him." I gave Lao Li ten minutes to 'beat it' to the frontier. If caught again dreadful things would happen. We would frizzle him alive and convert him into a Chinese ham! Lao Li passed hurriedly out of sight. I never saw or heard of him again.*

June 5th …All the gallantry had gone from poor Topsy and she was looking very tucked up. We pushed on – hour after hour – through the everlasting forest….I did not see a single bird all day. They seemed to have moved away at the coming of refugees….The rain came sweeping down as though it would last for ever and the shapes of clouds faded and formed and faded again in the dimness of the trees.

They passed through another relief camp. It appears there were still local guides with Gribble's group - *…The Duwa too was worried about the weather and anxious to return to his village. About midday the rain eased up but the wind was now blowing hard from the south-west and I came to the conclusion that we were no longer in Burma but were moving down the western slopes of the Patkai Mountain range in Assam, India. Nampong camp was about 6 to 8 miles distant.*

Numberless refugees and cattle had churned the sloping track into mud. The mud washed away by rain had left huge potholes in the track...Down the precipitous hillside other refugees were streaming in an endless line and disappearing into the forest at the bottom. The distant view showed no change – fold after fold of wooded hills, and it was through those hills that we would have to continue our journey to Ledo where there was a railway....

June 6ᵗʰ ...This morning I met a planter. He said he was leaving the next day on a visit to a supply dump at a place called Nam Zup at the foot of the hills about 20 miles distant. "You need only walk six miles to a little wayside camp at Yaman. From there we can pick up some elephants to take us down the mountain side to the river where you can get a 'country boat' to Margherita." I was much tempted by this kindly suggestion. "What about the monsoon?" I asked, "the river will be in flood." "It is early yet," he replied, "and 'country boats' are sure to be there." I consulted Ray who thought the scheme a good one. "We are very exhausted," he said "and our legs swollen and covered in sores. If we leave this nightmare trail we can ride on elephants, and sail comfortably into Margherita (near Ledo) in boats." It certainly did sound all right but we were soon to regret we ever left the mud trail for a journey that nearly brought us to complete destruction.....

I said goodbye to the Duwa with the fervently expressed hope that I would meet him again. "It is quite possible," I said, "that you will see me back in the Naga Hills as soon as the dry season sets in." Then with the exception of a few things we could ourselves carry we discarded all our belongings, and were ready for the last stage of our journey.

June 7ᵗʰ Our Planter friend H called for us at a very early hour. It was pouring with rain as we turned our backs on the muddy trail that led to Ledo and followed our new guides along a forest path that would bring us to the wayside camp at Yaman. "A European is there and in charge of the dump," H said, "he will put us up for the night. Tomorrow we can ride on the elephants."

The track was an uphill one until we reached a Naga village. Then came the descent I shall never forget. The side of the mountain was so steep as to have been necessary to cut out steps to enable the porters carrying supplies to the camp we had just left to get a foothold without slipping. Soon we were shut in the folds of the hills. The air became very humid. I was soon so hot and bothered that I found it necessary to keep my mind occupied by counting steps. I counted 3400 steps. When we eventually reached the foot of the ridge we walked for a while through dripping forest trees that towered over us in serried ranks. Then the steps began again but this time in an upward direction while the ocean of thick green trees continued to shut us in on all sides. H said the camp was on the top of the ridge we were climbing.

The steps seemed endless; and it was not till 1 p.m. that we reached a little encampment in a clearing. T was sitting in a bamboo hut over which had been thrown a waterproof tarpaulin. He was undoubtedly surprised to see us, but I could not hear what he said owing to the continuous patter of rain on the tarpaulin. ......the elephants had not made the usual journey up the mountain that day, and he did not know why, for no message had come. Perhaps the animals would arrive tomorrow. If so we could ride down the same afternoon to the river – a journey of four to five hours. I expressed my thanks but the thought that I might have to face those steps again made me feel ill.

T having to live all alone in that horrible jungle was as glad to see us as we were to see him: "I am afraid," he said, "I shall not be able to remain here many more days for the rain has been very heavy, and the mahouts now find it difficult to bring up the elephants. They will soon have to stop work."

The discussion continued. It was becoming uncertain whether it was going to be possible for them to use the elephants and the country boats. ..."*A nice lookout for us," I thought as I watched the rain pelting down outside, "in Burma the rivers are dangerously swollen by the middle of June, but perhaps here our luck will hold."*

June 8th   *"We have to walk a couple of miles to a little depot in order to meet the elephants," H said. "They cannot come to this place as it would be impossible for them to return to their river camp the same day."*

As we trudged through the jungle in dark overgrown places which for thousands of years had remained undisturbed, I felt a strange feeling of insecurity among those stately, wicked bearded trees which seemed to conspire with their long-clawed parasitical creepers to seize our clothing, and to scratch our hands and knees as if with an evil desire to obliterate us. The rain pattered down as hard as ever.

After walking for nearly two hours we came to some sheds in a clearing. The soggy drenched ground was churned into numerous muddy pits. This place was the elephant depot but there was no sign of

149

STORIES OF SURVIVAL IN BURMA

the supply elephants.

. ....finally H said he would go down the trail a little way and see if he could spot the elephant caravan. He had hardly disappeared round a bend in the track when he came running back waving his arms. The next moment the head of a large elephant appeared from out of the foliage quickly followed by others. As we jumped to our feet our faces lit up with joy. We were getting a move on at last.

(sfr)

I counted twenty elephants each with a mahout sitting on its neck and a load of two bags on its back. It did not take long to unload the bags and put ourselves on the elephants in readiness for the journey to the elephant camp. From my 'seat' on the broad bare back of an elephant I took a look at my friends who were already mounted on other elephants. The little Indian 'Chokra' seemed to be the only one who was enjoying himself. Then without any warning the elephants moved back down the trail.

As the great animals swayed and squelched through the mud and water I tried to adjust my balance to the rhythm of the elephant. For four long weary hours we slid, stumbled and slithered through yellow mud several feet deep. Sometimes the elephants sat on their behinds and slid down the precipitous track. Sometimes they went down on bended knees and dragged their hind legs forward one by one, and yet all the time we contrived to keep our 'seats'. I was amazed at the skill of these highly trained animals. I discovered that the mahout sitting in front of me on my elephant could speak a Kachin dialect (Jinghpaw) and presently he said to me, "Do you know that elephants used to be men? That is why they have so much intelligence!" He looked so serious when he said this that I almost believed him. "Thank God," I replied, "they now have four powerful legs otherwise our chances of getting out of this jungle would be remote." We both laughed and the people clinging to the other elephants wondered what there was to laugh at in such unsmiling surroundings.

As we neared the river at the foot of the mountain the jungle gave out a curiously damp smell like rotting vegetation, and the branches of the trees against which I brushed were chill and cold, their leaves like the limp and horribly thin hands of a dead man. Presently the mud trail came to an end at the edge of a stream full of dirty, yellow water.

The elephants plunged into the stream which twisted and turned, and was full of rocks and many fallen trees. As we approached the junction of the stream with the parent river at Nam Zup the water became considerably deeper. I remember asking the mahout if there were any boats at the camp. He said, "I have not seen any for some days but there might be some at a place six miles lower down. The Sahib stationed at Nam Zup went away in a hurry yesterday and has taken twenty elephants with him. There is no one in the camp except a Gurkha headman and a few coolies." This news was not only alarming but unaccountably mysterious. "What has happened?" I thought. I looked back and saw H sitting very dejectedly on his elephant.

The elephants were now up to their bellies in water. When we reached the Nam Zup river we had to cross to the opposite bank in order to reach the camp. Tucking our legs under our chins we clung to the elephants as they half paddled half swam their way through the swiftly flowing water to some bamboo huts on the river bank.

The camp looked horribly desolate and depressing. We would have to camp at this place, Nam Zup for the night. We landed on the river bank caring little for our appearance. "I expected to meet Mac here," said H "but he left a note to say he received information about a large number of refugees in distress at a mountain pass, one hundred miles to the north east. Mac has gone out with twenty elephants to try and locate them. He will be gone a long time and I shall have to stay at this dump to look after things. "And the boats?" I suggested. "There are none," he replied, "The rains have set in heavily and the boatmen have cleared off to Margherita. However there is an officer at Simon, about five hours' march from here, and some elephants will take you there tomorrow. You may get a boat there. Anyway it is worth trying."

June 9th Their plans had become very uncertain. There was to be much more riding on the back of elephants. *I said goodbye to H and we set off for the place called Simon, six miles down river on the right bank of the Namhpuk Hka. It was a link the chain of supply dumps which had been formed to get food to the refugees' relief camps in the hills. Now the rains had come some of these supply dumps were to be closed down owing to the impossibility of keeping open communications during the rains.*

We reached the camp at Simon after a ride of 52 hours through everlasting forest swamps. I was so stiff that it was only with difficulty that I could get off the bare back of the elephant. We felt extraordinary relief to find M still there, and to learn that there were some country boats available. "All the boats have gone except four," said M, "which I held back to take me out of this. I have closed down the depot. You can have two of the boats. It will take you two days to reach Margherita." I was overcome with grateful thanks.

The camp itself was a dismal place and full of flies, but I slept soundly, with the comforting thought that we were nearing our journey's end – a strange ghastly journey that started on the 4th May.

June 10th It was cold and wet as a sea fog as we got into our little dugouts early this morning. Ray and I were in one and Burua and the chokra in the other. The river was grey in colour with a fast current, and we soon found that it contained a series of acute bends and fierce rapids. A boat boy stood at either end of the little craft and held a long bamboo in his two hands.

That journey will remain with me till I die. Once in mid-stream all power was swept from us. This age-old river with its grass islands, released from the leanness of the dry season was enjoying itself. We were carried to some rapids where the large, white-crested waves jostled us, hurled us to their friends, treated us in a hurly-burly manner and slopped pailfulls of themselves into our craft.

We lurched and groaned and bumped in a giddy, nonsensical drunken dance while the boat-boys screamed at each other. We got through one rapid only to run into others. Twice my gunwale went under and righted itself, leaving us to sit in a mud bath. Then we hurled round a bend at terrific speed, and I got ready to jump. "Pole," shouted the boy from the rear and the boy in front 'poled' and was lucky to find bottom. We negotiated that bend with beating hearts.

There was then a period of comparative calm until rounding another bend we saw in front of us the fiercest of all rapids. The boys jumped into the water up to their waists and pushed the boat to some shallows. We got out and hanging on to the boat, half lifted and half dragged it away from the rapids over a sort of pebbly beach until the rapids were behind us. After this all went well until we reached the junction of the mighty Muganton river which we could see was in spate, and rushing to join our river in a maddening white torrent. We ran our boat to the river bank to get our breath for the next round.

The water was intensely rough, choppy and dirty as we pushed the nose of the boat against the current. Quickly and violently we were seized by a swirl of the water and carried rapidly to the opposite bank.

Now this might well have been the end of this chronicle for right ahead of us was a gigantic tree, perhaps a hundred and fifty feet long, lying half in the water, its root upended on the river bank. Our little craft was swept straight towards the timber and there was nothing we could do to avoid it. The boat-boys were quick to notice that the trunk of the tree was slightly arched, and managed to steer the boat to this gap between tree and water. We lay flat in the boat which shot under the tree and out the other side without a scratch, thankful to be alive.

After this uncanny escape the river widened and deepened. The boat-boys called it the Biri Dihing (the head waters of the Brahmaputra river.) The sun came out, and we lay back in the boat and dozed in the sunlight. About dusk we reached a little Kachin village and sought refuge in the headman's house. The name of the village is Ning-gam and I remember there was such a village in the Hukawng Valley. The people here tell me that their parents had migrated from the Hukawng. They like their present abode because it is nearer to civilization. Only one day's journey by boat to Margherita where there is a good market. This news is like music to our ears.

June 11ᵗʰ Rain was falling very heavily and delayed our departure. But we were anxious to get on, so I had the two boats lashed together and a waterproof canvas carried by the boat-boys for covering cargo thrown over a framework of bamboo. It kept the rain off us and about 5 p.m. we landed near the railway bridge at Margherita and made our way to the Rest Camp in pouring rain.

Now this particular chronicle is done. But I hope to complete the story in the not too distant future when I am restored in mind and body, with beard shorn off and clothed to look like a human being again. Some of my friends will never return, for they died on this the most extraordinary trek in history – a trek that caused untold suffering to thousands of people of many nationalities. Yes, how they suffered, young and old alike. It is astounding that so many survived and it shows in startling fashion the extent of human endurance when up against it.

Topsy gets a paragraph to herself. She arrived safely in Ledo and found a comfortable home. She may have forgotten her former master but he, at any rate, would like to renew his wanderings with his old friend Topsy – when the time is ripe.

CHAPTER TWENTY FOUR

'...*God in his mercy had ended it...*'
Josephine's news about the children.

In early June Dr Russell and Captain Gribble and their fellow travellers had survived their journeys to India. In May Josephine had reached Calcutta where there was a network of missionaries to greet her. But most of her large family were very far away in England. During the following months the only entries she wrote in her diary were bits of news she heard about the children from whom she had got separated. From various accounts it seems that some survived and some tragically perished in the Hukawng Valley along with Lillian Bald and John Derry and some of the military.

While still climbing high mountains in May she had thought about the group, with Myitkyina airfield under threat. She probably didn't know at this point that the Japanese took the airfield on May 8th and that her group had not managed to get on a plane. *May 17th. We heard news for the first time for nearly three weeks. The Japanese were in Myitkyina on the 6th having come unexpectedly, not up the railway or the Irrawaddy, but overland from the east....the schoolgirls with John and Lillian had come to Myitkyina on the hospital train on the 3rd. They would not have arrived before the 4th....2 days to get away.*

Another diary entry tells of the bombing raids causing chaos at the airfield: *The hospital train from Katha reached Myitkyina on the evening of May 4th, and with hundreds of other evacuees, our party waited on the airfield for a plane. On the 6th they were still there and were scattered by an air raid. Later in the day a plane was brought for the, 'Bishop's Home children' – they were called. But they were some distance away and some of them were very small. When they arrived the plane had gone. It would have been folly for the pilot to wait long. In any case he would have soon had as many passengers as he could take. But the Japanese were almost there and all the refugees had to be ordered out of the town. They went in military lorries or on foot. Our party was taken to the hundred and second mile where the way divides. From there the older girls and boys with Lillian Bald and John Derry and a few other adults began the trek along the Hukawng valley. Two military men accompanied them.*

She also wrote: *So we waited and on October 15th we received definite information. The smaller children were being sheltered at Sumprabum in Upper Burma, and although they were safe, they could not be brought through until after the war.* Sumprabum lies east of the Hukawng Valley.

Old photo *'On the Sumprabum Road'*   (dml)

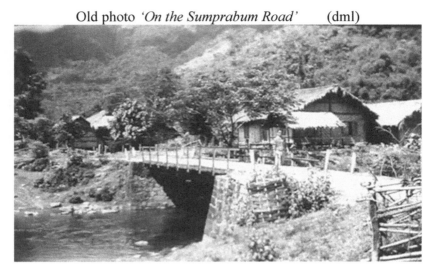

And she added more details another time. She appears to have spoken with Eileen, the oldest child. *The smaller children, thirty in all, were taken by lorry to Sumprabum thirty miles in the other direction. They stayed in the PWD bungalow in Sumprabum, and the military, before they left, gave them 70 bags of rice. An Irish Roman Catholic priest, Fr. Stuart, who was there was given money also to help them. For a month they lived in comparative comfort, but on the 15th June Chinese troops arrived and took all the food they could find. Mrs D who with her own four children was there also, managed to hide a few sacks. But she took fright and decided to trek to India with her children and two or three other adults.*

Fr. Stuart took the other children to a village two miles away and cared for them there for three months. They were in the care of one of Fr. Stuart's Jinghpaw Christians and were comparatively well fed all the time. But Fr. Stuart himself had other work to do in Ki's large district and often he was away. Three of the children died in those three months. Twelve-year old Eileen, being the senior of the party by three years, seems to have mothered them all. 'We were a long way from the stream,' she told me, 'and it was cold. So we did not bathe much, and we had no clothes to change so they were not washed at all.'

In July the Japanese came, but they did not interfere. In fact they gave the children food now and then, and Eileen had a blanket and pullover that a Japanese soldier gave her.

'We were singing hymns one day,' she told me. 'And the Japanese soldier came along to listen. He knew English a little and said he was not a Christian but had been in a Mission school and knew those hymns.' Another day they heard him singing: 'Jesus loves me, this I know, For the Bible tells me so.' On September 10 two British officers arrived from Putao, eighty miles away. They promised food which was dropped by plane five days later. On October 5 they brought elephants and took them all away. They arrived in Putao on the 13th where they bathed and were given clean clothes! From there they were taken by plane to Assam.

But then a telegram came; twenty three small children had arrived in Assam. I was sent to Gauhati to meet them, and found them in a better physical condition than any evacuees I had seen. Some had had malaria and were not very fit, many had sores, but they were lively and very talkative. They were surprised to see me. 'Somebody told us you were dead,' was the cheery greeting of one child. I responded, for they did not seem to have grasped the real tragedy of it all;

'I walked all the way,' I said 'and raced you even though you came on an aeroplane.' We brought them to Calcutta. Eventually they went to a well organised Burma evacuee camp in Bangalore in S.India. There survives an old photo of about twenty children on the back of which Josephine herself has written *'Children from Bishop's Home in India'.*

Later in November she wrote again about the other group: *All Souls' Day. We waited four and a half months hearing rumours and scraps of news now and then. Two thousand people were held up in the Hukawng valley at a place called Shingbwiyang, on the other side of a river unfordable in the rains. The track too was knee-deep in mud. The RAF was keeping them supplied with food and after the rains they would come through, we were told. Our children were probably in that camp.*

And finally she added: *There were thirty-six in the party which began the trek with the two soldiers. There was little food and on some days they had practically none. On the way were many other refugees in the same plight: malaria, dysentery, cholera, exposure, exhaustion. And they slept in the jungle at night in the pouring rain. The day came when they could go no longer and they stayed in a village while the two soldiers went on to get help. One died on the way and the other arrived exhausted, but before help could be sent back, an Indian soldier from Burma arrived in the camp. He had passed through that village at the end of August, he said ... ...It was too long a journey for school girls in the Hukawng valley in the rainy season. God in his mercy had ended it.*

Josephine ended her diary with these words.

There were other reports. On September 20th a letter was written from Shingbwiyang by the Assistant Superintendent, Hukawng Valley, C E Darlington: '... *Six pathetic specimens arrived, one of whom has since died. Included in the six was the last remaining girl out of 75 Bishop's Home girls who reached Yupang, and two teachers out of a staff of eight*..... (letter addressed to G E D Walker, Political Officer, Margherita, and forwarded for information to R M Thomson, Refugee Administrator Officer, Margherita)

And in a report written from Shingbwiyang dated Sept 26th and signed by A C Munroe there is a record of some Anglo-Indians who arrived on the 24th including two teachers from the Bishop Home School, Rangoon – Mrs C D' Silva and Miss Newton, and a pupil Miss Hilda Millan. None of these names appear on the nominal roll of Burma refugees who entered India by routes leading to Margherita, Assam.

When refugees arrived at Margherita and other Tea-planters' camps their names were recorded. There are many thousands of sad omissions from these lists of refugees. The story of the children is one of many tragedies where the details about what happened can never be fully known.

CHAPTER TWENTY FIVE
May – June

Heroes and Villains, the story of Benjamin Katz

'...but I was a madman in those days,   I simply pushed the guns aside....'

Back in January Captain Gribble had written: '...*From the large Shan village of Mainghkwan which is the centre of the universe in the Hukawng, tracks radiate in all directions.   But the one that we shall be more than interested in runs north to the Chindwin river (Tanai Hka) at Taihpa, and thence to Yupbang, a village on the banks of the Tarung Hka – river of death – 8 miles further on.*
   In the dry season there are raft ferries at the crossing of both these rivers.   The track then turns west and continues another 25 miles until it reaches the dreary little Kachin village of Shingbwiyang at the foot of the eastern range of the Naga hills...
Shingbwiyang was the last village on the track before the great climbs began over the Patkai range of mountains. On June 9th the jungle track was so bad that refugees were to become stranded here for an indefinite period of time. There were two exceptional individuals who stayed and helped the refugees in this desolate, disease-ridden, overcrowded place. They worked untiringly until September when, much weakened by illness, they too had to face the exhausting journey on foot to India. They were Neil North, a young political officer, and Sgt. Benjamin Katz, a RAMC Orderly.
   Among surviving records is a remarkable *'Letter from Shingbwiyang'* that Katz wrote to 'Ted'. In this frank and shocking letter we can glimpse Katz's extreme frustration and bloody minded determination and courage in the face of awful circumstances.
   He had arrived at Shingbwiyang with other soldiers after a journey that was similar to that of many others. This was the day before Dr Russell arrived.   Katz wrote: '...*the Gurkhas are a great crowd!   The date was May 12th, in the evening.   We decided to rest on the morrow as the next part of the journey was climbing. We had a full view of the hills from here.   They appeared grand as scenery, but hell – it looked a mighty tough proposition!...That day we saw planes dropping rations, our first time.   I was fascinated....I estimated the crowd to be well over 1000 in number.   I saw only one man distributing food. It was a hell of a job. We volunteered to help for a couple of hours, keeping the crowd in line. Sometimes force was necessary.*

Cholera had broken out here in Shingbwiyang but as far as I could see, no medical help of any sort was available, although a number of doctors had passed through. Not one of them would stay over to help....I learnt that the man in charge of the camp was C.W. ("Neil") North of the Burma Frontier Service. It seems to me Ted, that this fellow was the only one to stay at his post...

Now Ted, here is the strangest part of the story – something I cannot explain – but I feel sure you will understand even though others are certain to discredit it. You know of course how things are between Brenda and me. Well, perhaps it really was telepathy, but I seemed to hear her voice: "You are staying Bunny, aren't you? You can help here, really help!" And somehow the cholera epidemic didn't seem so frightening. I felt that I would never get malaria. How could dysentery touch me if I were to take care of myself – and so on....everyone, North included, thought that the evacuation would be finished in a week or less. The Japs would by now have closed the last door of escape to India. The stream of refugees would soon dry up...And so we settled down to work, from early-morning till late at night, with hardly time to eat or even wash. ...Jones too was ill but refused to lie down. He still did his full share. How he stood on his feet was a miracle.

North very wisely gave us a full hand and I'm sure he was satisfied with the results. Two of us would stay on guard in the ration godown at night, a Tommy gun ready in the event of an emergency and the third member slept in North's bungalow. The male refugees never once considered the women and kids, so we had to use force to get them into the front of the queue, but on the whole it was not too hard a job keeping them all in line.

Captain Gribble arrived here on May 16th. He had written: *'The glow in the western sky lit up the outline of the hills – the Naga Hills – but the sight of them caused a stir of uneasiness for from now on the track would traverse those broken and precipitious forest-clad hills for one hundred miles or more!'*

Katz was overwhelmed with the situation and the thought probably did not cross his mind that on all routes out of Burma members of the military forces were under pressure to avoid the many illnesses raging through the camps – no easy task when water sources were often polluted, and much of the available space was occupied by sick people. At all costs soldiers had to try to keep themselves fit enough for the task ahead of defending India from the Japanese.

The military were the worst offenders! Officers came barging up the steps of the godown with no consideration for anybody else. One of them – I think he was a Colonel – was too demanding and even insulting. I kicked him down the steps! What else could I do, Ted? This was no ordinary situation....refugees were dying of cholera, dysentery, malaria or exhaustion. As there were no volunteers to do the burying, men for this job were chosen at the point of the gun. North certainly went the right way about things.

Katz wrote that around May 16th a letter arrived asking for Neil to help at the Yupang ferry, as it was chaos there and he spoke fluent Kachin. He agreed Katz should accompany him. '*...North and I left the following morning. He marches at high speed so at times I simply could not keep up with him...The same scenes greeted us mile after mile – the dead and dying, that horrible stench, the heartbreaking sight of women and kids plastered with mud, stumbling and wading through slowly and so pathetically. I dropped out on the last stretch for a rest and arrived at the ferry after nightfall. I felt too sick to sleep.*

The situation here was serious. Some had drowned through overcrowding the boats; the jungle rope spanning the river had been broken during a squabble. It would take weeks to replace. North soon gave the natives the confidence they needed... So the three of us, North, Arnold and I stayed on duty at the ferry throughout the day. During the whole time we were there not one life was lost through drowning.....The military caused the most trouble. One C.O. of a large party of soldiers attempted to commandeer the boats, even though he was quite aware of the fact that almost 1000 civilians including many women and children had arrived hours before him. He calmed down a little when Arnold told him who he was....it was here at the crossing that I first came into contact with McGuire, the Deputy Commissioner. He stayed to work at the ferry. He also spoke Kachin.

After helping here for a while Katz returned to Shingbwiyang. '*...Just as I entered the village I called over to someone I recognized. He replied: "See you in a minute, after I have buried this corpse!" We went over to North's bungalow. North was still away on duty and the scene here added to my miserable mood. Though the house was full of officers, the place was in a filthy state. Poor Neil! It was not fair that his house should be ransacked in this way – and he, the only officer to stay at his post. Personal boxes had been broken open, food, clothes and even* *money had been stolen. I spoke my mind – by evening the place was comparatively shipshape. Each person promised to clean his own bed-space.*

The food position was critical and there were no medicines available. Of course, there was no doctor either – only an R.A.M.C. orderly – C.

McGuire fell ill with high fever. So did Lakis Thompson, Bickford and Arnold's servant. I spent most of my time nursing these people.....A letter from North arrived in which he said he would be back on June 8ᵗʰ or 9ᵗʰ. Arnold and McGuire decided to stay in this camp until North's arrival...I took on the job of rationing. But there was insufficient food to go round. How people survived at this period was a miracle. The women came to the door, crying for nourishment for their children. I felt like crying myself!

A bogus doctor caused some trouble by selling useless powder in the camp at high prices. I caught him red-handed on two occasions but could do nothing as he was treating the officers of the bungalow for mud sores on their feet and charging nothing. No one would listen to my accusations...

... Now came bad news! The Chinese army of 4000 men were heading this way and with the food position as it was, this meant trouble with a capital "T". However this particular time there was no looting and he made the comment - '*...No looting at this stage, thank God!'*

I was surprised to hear that all the officials had decided not to await North's arrival; that the situation was hopeless and that they would leave on the 5ᵗʰ June. At this time there were about 400 refugees here and very little food.

McGuire and Arnold wrote a letter to the Government in India explaining the position. A picking-up device was set up on the ration field. If a fighter plane happened to pass over, there was a good chance of the letter being picked up.

Katz included a copy of the letter in his own. It was headed – '*Most urgent! Shingbwiyang: 1ˢᵗ June 1942 and was from R.E.M.McGuire ICS Deputy Commissioner, Myitkyina, and R.B.Arnold ICS, Finance Secretary, Burma. To Chief Civil Officer: Government of Assam, Ledo.'*

Here are extracts from the letter: '*The following gives brief details of present evacuation position in Hukawng Valley route (including both Mogaung – Mainghkwan and Myitkyina – Mainghkwan and immediate and vital requirements, if slow death from starvation, exposure and illness is not to overtake some of 2000 people, mainly women and children, most of whom are families of Gurkha soldiers and many others, also Indian and Anglo Indian Government servants*…There were descriptions of the flooded rivers, and how evacuees had been advised to stay where they were during the monsoon till about September/October. There were lists of foodstuffs and basic medical supplies that were needed. '*…injections which can only be administered by a doctor are not suggested…*'

The letter goes on to say there had now been more arrivals, with more expected. '*…Except for tea, salt and small balance of last night's milk and rice, this camp has NO RATIONS AT ALL.* There were also requests for a food drop further along the route for those who were planning to travel. '*…add following drugs and equipment for a hospital which has been opened under an RAMC Orderly who has volunteered to stay for duration of rains. His medical knowledge is elementary and we earnestly request that a properly constituted medical unit be sent with the utmost despatch possible. All efforts to obtain volunteers from doctors evacuating have been a dismal failure. In the meanwhile there is no alternative but to accept the offer of the Medical Orderly (C) who may kill some people through unskilled use of the drugs. But with him the sick will stand some chance….*

'*…It is difficult to advise evacuees whether to undertake the journey or to calculate rations and equipment to be carried, without knowledge following details.* There was a request for information to be dropped about camps, available shelter, food rations, medical help, epidemics, maps and possible transport.

In the final section of the letter the dire situation was described with unsolved dilemmas. '*…All administrations, including Medical Officers especially appointed to this route, with the honourable exception of Neil North, have deserted their posts. Such organisations as have been improvised are being done by a few personal officers. McGuire, one of the signatories to this letter, has gone down with a fever (malaria?) And Bickford shows signs of going down. This will shortly be the case of everyone, in the absence of a balanced diet, properly cooked food and skilled medical attention. The majority of evacuees who will have any chance of getting out during the rains will have left Shingbwiyang during the next five days and subject to the requests made in this letter being met, we feel that we shall then have done all we reasonably can. On 6th June therefore the last volunteer officer (except the medical orderly) will leave if they are fit to travel.*

Neil North will probably be advised by us to leave. Since one officer with no servants, police or medical attendant would be a sacrifice in vain. Whether he will comply with this advice is not known. At present he is away at Taipor. If, however, the Government of Assam will accept the proposal being made by Wilkie ICS Commissioner, Sagaing Division, now in transit to Ledo to take over the Hukawng Valley as far as Shingbwiyang and send at once an organized expedition to establish an outpost here, we have no doubt that Neil North would certainly stay on. Signed R.E.McGuire, F.B.Arnold.

After quoting this letter in full, Katz commented: *'This then was the letter composed, to be picked up by plane. I'll confess to feeling hurt. Although Arnold and McGuire were both aware of my intentions of staying behind. I felt that I'd done a bigger share of the work up to now; yet my name was not even mentioned. They left me out in the cold. I mentioned nothing about this. I did not share in their belief that the position was hopeless. If food was to be dropped, we could be the means of saving a large number of lives, even if it was on the cards that some of us would die of disease, surely this was something to die for – an ideal. We had already been the means of saving many lives, why give up now. I intended to see the job finished or die in the attempt. Brave thoughts, foolishness, or whatever you care to think, Ted. I saw no other course open to me.*

On June 5th all left for India in wretched weather. Only C and I remained behind in the bungalow to carry on the work for the refugees. As far as the people in the camps were concerned I was now the Commandant. The beard had brown to a good length – I looked older – I thought I would pass as "the authority". Anyhow it was worth a try!

I was well aware of the fact that I'd taken on a tremendous responsibility....One hour after the party had left, I went down with malaria. But it was impossible for me to lie down in bed however. Crowds were coming to the bungalow begging for food, crying and cursing, as if I was to blame for their predicament. It was awful! I couldn't sleep a wink that night I felt so miserable.'

He continued to describe the desperate conditions. *'...People died like flies. I followed North's policy of forcing people to bury the bodies – at the point of a rifle.....More Chinese were now coming into the village looting food.....And I had to go out time and time again to stop them. None of the refugees helped me. Sometimes the blessed Chinese stuck guns into my ribs when I told them to get out of our huts. But I was a madman in those days. I simply pushed the guns aside. I could not prevent some looting....*

...Neil North was now overdue: it worried me. The Chinese commander called at my bungalow to discuss the situation. They saw for themselves we had no store of food, but we dared not even show a grain of rice. They would take anything. I advised them to push on to the river at Yupang, 23 miles from here, where there was sufficient rice to feed all their blessed army. So for two days we discussed the situation and drew maps.

Something happened on the second day that almost turned my hair grey. We could eat nothing, as we dared not show our limited supply of rice, and during a conversation with the Chinese Commander my houseboy entered the room and asked if I wanted rice with my lunch!

C often used bad language and did not care what he said about the Chinese even in their presence. Once, while I was trying to convince the Chinese of the advisability of a move, C barged in and began chatting to the Commander and playing about with a loaded revolver. All of a sudden there was a loud report and a bullet creased the commander's nose. Holy Smoke! What would have happened if the Commander had been killed?

A plane dropped rations, and Katz managed to get the Chinese to assist with moving and guarding the rice. '*...The Chinese left the following morning. The main body were quite orderly, but the stragglers gave some trouble. One party sneaked into my bungalow and tried to shoot me. I had the Tommy gun loaded and ready...* '

Katz asked C to show him around the hospital. '*...On making inquiries I found out that C took little interest in the hospital but simply loved to bully. His language was abominable, especially to the women. Immediately I organized a party to transfer the living to better quarters. The hospital was burnt and I gave C a good hiding...* '

He found some refugees willing to help, but some were troublemakers. '*...Up to now I'd had no news of Neil North. Chinese stragglers passing through tried to loot, but we managed to stop most of them. My fever was down but C got a bad attack. While cooking some food I had an accident. A nail went through my plimsoll and clean through my right foot. This laid me up. I could not possibly stand and as luck would have it, I could not manage to get down to the field when a ration plane dropped a small amount of food.*

He described how some refugees looted the food, but some helped.

There was a Mrs Doran – *'..Mrs Doran did wonders as far as I know during the whole of the evacuation. She was the only woman who really did help. She even carried many heavy food sacks throughout the day.*

Odd Chinese parties passed the bungalow daily and entered with intentions to loot. The Tommy gun held them off. I had no peace day or night. It was this danger that gave me the idea of the Union Jack. Miss Baker (who also helped a great deal) made one from odd cloth. This flag was destined to be our saviour in the days to come. The food position had become extremely critical. I was beginning to lose hope. People were actually dying of starvation.

(sfr)

A party of starving Chinese came to the bungalow while I was out inspecting the huts in the village and I returned to find the bungalow surrounded by Chinese – some with rifles and machine guns. Baxter had refused them entry, brave fellow, and was gallantly holding the fort until my arrival. They had an interpreter, thank heaven and I quickly explained the position. But they demanded food. The situation looked ugly but was slightly eased when we produced some bulls for them.....I saw some Chinese officers looking at the Union Jack flying over the bungalow and it gave us the idea of bluffing in order to get rid of them. So I told them that this was a military base. Our soldiers were out in the hills looking for the Japs and would be returning soon. As this Chinese party insisted on staying on the compound, I hinted on how annoyed our

soldiers would be to find strangers in their quarters. They only stayed the night, but in the compound and even underneath the bungalow, it was like sleeping on a volcano. They left early in the morning. The relief I felt was almost painful....Neil North had not yet arrived and nor had he sent word. I now gave him up as lost!

The noise of a plane got us all out into the open. It was a fighter. I immediately put out the signal for food. The pilot dropped a message asking if we were the Chinese army. I replied, yes! Anything to get food dropped on us! It was not such a big lie and I was probably doing a good turn to the Chinese who were doubtlessly following up. We also managed to attract attention to the message waiting to be picked up. Another message was dropped, telling us that the pilot would return to pick up the message and that food would be dropped that very day. You can imagine our excitement. Hope at long last!...'. Group Captain David Roberts of the R.A.F. was the pilot. This was the message: 'Ok message received. Are you Chinese army? (to which I replied, yes!) I know what you mean, but I'm sorry I have no bloody hook to pick it up with. Tell the Chinese I have got their message and if the weather holds out, the Americans will drop tons of rice for them. I will send one of our chaps to bring you some rations this afternoon. My love to the girl in the red frock. Good luck!'

And he was as good as his word! Can you imagine our joy Ted, at seeing this food being dropped as if from heaven. We shouted. We sang and danced – and cried!

However, the situation was getting worse, if that was possible. A new message was about to arrive which when Katz read it must have increased his feeling of isolation. The vital food drops were often made impossible because of thick mist and rain clouds over the jungle, and there was advice to all at the camp to stay and not attempt to move on. However there was also conflicting advice to whoever was in charge to attempt to move on and travel on other unspecified and presumably unknown routes.

Later on the following message was dropped. The contents puzzled me somewhat (it was dated 9th June): "To Mr C.W.North – Assistant Superintendent, or if absent any other Gazetted Officer at Shingbwiyang. 1. Orders should be given to all refugees at Shingbwiyang, that they must not at present attempt to proceed further. The Namyung river was reported unfordable on 5th June and the depth of mud on the Pangsau

Pass track makes porterage impossible. 600 persons were reported on the 7th June held up at Tagap Ga, unable to go forward. The camp organization between Namyung river and Pangsau is withdrawing to Nampong as it cannot be rationed. The existence of rations along the road between Shingbwiyang and Nampong cannot therefore be guaranteed. This journey now takes about 10 days even if the river can be crossed. Efforts will be made to cross and when possible to drop rations at Shingbwiyang, but weather conditions may preclude this for periods of several days and enemy action from the air may prevent it entirely.
2. Any officers at Shingbwiyang (other than North, to whom separate instructions have been issued by General Broad) now have no further duties to perform. They should if physically fit and have necessary porters available, leave by any route alternative to the Pangsau Pass which North considers feasible. They are advised to seek assistance of parties of the Chinese Fifth army, now presumed arriving at Shingbwiyang, to continue the journey to India.
Signed: E.T.D.Lambert
C.F.B.Pearce

Katz described his reaction to this message. *'Hell! I was hoping that officials would be sent through to help me and instead of that, India was withdrawing them. The joke was that they had already gone off! Well, I'd manage somehow with God's help! The refugees would not be left to their fate. I might succeed where all the higher officials failed.*

There were more rations dropped and some desperate refugees would take the food and run away.'*...I found another two helpers who later proved so valuable in running the camp. One was Wakefield and the other a Gurkha Jemadar, who was the means of convincing the other Gurkhas of the sincerity of our motives in storing the food. We worked till well after midnight...My foot was still giving me trouble but I managed to get around.'*

There was a terrible story from the jungle. *'Some Kachins had now returned from the jungles and we heard how the Chinese have treated them. The poor devils had been tied to stakes. Some were killed. All the livestock had been taken. Their paddys had been destroyed and every available untensil stolen. Also their knives (dahs) without which these jungle people cannot survive. I tried to get them to look for North but they were too scared of the Chinese who were known to be in that vicinity.*

'Nine Japanese fighters flew over the village roof tops trying to find out what was happening…..' **Katz**

Katz was attempting to run the camp with almost no help. He urgently needed to make contact with Neil North from whom he had not heard any news for some time. The threat from the Chinese was increasing and completely wearing him out.

'..I stayed up throughout the night compiling a new message to be picked up by the fighter. In the morning I asked Jemadar Gam Bahadur to try for volunteers to search for North at Yupang and Taihpa. Some Gurkhas promised to start on the following day...' The Chinese – *'... had very cunningly banded themselves together, fifty-strong and every man armed with a rifle....It was useless attempting to do anything at that stage...Later with Gam Bahadur's help, we checked up on our strength; twenty-six rifles, one Tommy gun (with 40 rounds) and two revolvers.*

I planned to disarm the Chinese at the first available moment...a questionnaire was dropped addressed to North. Lots of questions were asked. I must confess some were "double Dutch" to me. I learnt with joy that the Government were definitely interested in Shingbwiyang.

Some more Kachins called at the bungalow. As two spoke Burmese, I asked Wakefield to get hold of their story. Maybe we could entice them back to the village. Labour was urgently needed! In the middle of this "pow-wow" Neil North walked into the bungalow! Never in all my life have I been so glad to see anyone – and to think I had almost given him up for lost!

This was June 17th. Neil looked in bad shape, however, and hadn't eaten for two whole days. It had been a hell of a journey getting here. North told me later that he had expected to find the Chinese in his bungalow, so that to see the Union Jack flying was a very big moment indeed. I could not get North to rest just then, except to have a meal. There was the questionnaire to fill in...'

This was done and to their relief it was picked up by a plane. Neil went down with a fever, and Katz commented – *'...I had thought of nursing him during the night, but no sooner did my head touch the pillow and I went fast asleep – the first peaceful sleep for many days.'*

North soon started organizing the camp.'*...We co-operated well together. Never once during the whole period of the evacuation did we* *have a row. A doctor – Major B (retired) from Maymyo and his family arrived. Also a Captain from the KOYLI'S – Y was his name. He was accompanied by a Staff Sergeant S of the royal Engineers and it looked as it we were now to have some real help.*

Unfortunately later events proved otherwise. Largely due to North's efforts, a small police force was organized. Gurkha sentries were appointed and a weekly ration system for the refugees was introduced.

There was trouble with Captain Y who tried to bribe Katz into giving him tinned food. Later when ready to leave against advice he contracted fever. Some medical supplies were dropped but Major B started charging people money for injections and death certificates.

There was news of the approaching Chinese army. An advance party of about 800 arrived. It was an explosive situation – '*…We concealed the whereabouts of our food store…We dared not distribute food to the refugees, no matter how hungry they were. One rifle shot and I'm sure the village would have gone up in flames….The problem was easily solved. They simply ate and ate, day and night. In our possession were maps and information written in Chinese for this Army's benefit. They were duly handed over. But instead of obeying the instructions and moving off to the spot where the Americans were dropping loads of rice for them, the devils just ate – and many died through overeating…*'

The problems with the Chinese continued. Katz had had malaria a few times but he found it impossible to rest. He usually supervised the food dropping and distribution, but there was a time when he felt too ill.

'*…I was feeling extremely groggy and on fire with a high temperature, and I could not take my usual commanding position on the field.*

Some Indians looted. The Chinese ran off with loads and some of the Anglos, especially Major B, knowing that I was feeling ill, took advantage and helped themselves. The task of regaining order was too much for me. The world spun round and I collapsed in a heap. Some Indians carried me to the bungalow…But this time I had a very high fever and was forced to bed. North took good care of me… I knew I was dying and North was very alarmed. The Colonel in charge of the Medical Unit of the Chinese army was informed by North and it was due to this doctor that I pulled through. He had the proper medicine….I believe that the doctor's name was Colonel Jennin. He had taken his degree at Edinburgh and Germany. I was the most fortunate of people and will not forget it…'

'*… Major L and Captain H who were liaison officers to the Chinese*

Army, broke off all relations with the army and asked to be fed and housed by us. Captain H proved very troublesome, wanting everything he set his eyes on. It did not look as if he would be much help to us. Major L backed him up.

'...I'd like to say a word here about the R.A.F. Excepting during the May to June period, we were never once let down. And though at times we only had one day's ration in hand, the food came through. During mid-June and the whole of July, the monsoon was generally heavy. Rain and mist covered everything, so that we could barely see the tops of the trees. Yet by some miracle or rather by super expert piloting, the R.A.F. broke through and dropped those precious stores – not once or twice, but on dozens of occasions. I take off my hat to those chaps, expecially to Pilot Officer David Lord!'

The story continued. Many died of cerebral malaria. Katz was ill through July but carried on working. The camp was well organized. Kachins had returned and helped with collecting and storing food. *'...Many incidents occurred during June and July....Nine Japanese fighters flew over the village roof tops trying to find out what was happening...'*

'...So many incidents Ted, that I cannot hope to include, although they are of interest. But the story I simply must tell! While the Chinese were here, four dogs appeared as if from nowhere. Each took up a position at the door of one bungalow. If any Chinese set foot in the compound, the dogs promptly went for him. Even General Tu was attacked, but we deemed it wise to stop the dogs before any damage was done to him. Where the dogs were fed, I don't know. They refused our food. Still they kept a vigil for 24 hours a day. Even now I cannot understand how this miracle came about...'

'...We were fortunate in getting hold of Bim Bahadur, who Neil North knew at Sumprabum. This chap though encumbered with a large family, proved the most valuable and trusted helper of them all...'

Katz was now very thin, his legs gave him trouble and he was constantly getting a high fever. *'...North had to go to Hkalak on August 17th to discuss the situation with Lambert, the political officer who had come down from India for information....Major B the doctor died.'*

North sent word back to Shingbwiyang that the Government had appointed Katz Refugee Officer. Once again Katz was nursed through illness, with Amar Singh an S.A.S. arriving and helping look after him. Then a letter came through that Katz had been appointed Assistant

Superintendent in the Burma Frontier Service as from August 3rd. *'...This was a big rise in the world for me, and I suppose I would now be released from the army. I hope so! This good news bucked me up tremendously. Brenda will be delighted!*

Some people left to walk on further and there were more deaths. *'...We now heard that relief was on its way. Darlington of the Frontier Service; Munro, a refugee officer, Captain Weymouth an RAMC doctor and 50 soldiers had started out from Margherita. North and I were down with fever. I sometimes doubted if we would ever get of of this valley of death...North told me to make my way to India before it was too late. I refused! We would sink or swim together!...Evan Darlington was the very man to relieve North, as he understood the refugees...we prepared for the journey...*

Well the evacuation was now almost over. We had seen most of the refugees on their way. I estimated that we had helped some 40,000 people on to India but of course I may be wrong in my calculations. I've not been able to get the official figure as yet. It was left to Darlington and Munro to put the finishing touches to it. It had not been a pleasant job and I got very little gratitude for my pains. Perhaps it was because fear and greed were the dominant feelings of most of the refugees. Whatever they saw, they wanted but we had to store things away for a rainy day (we had many rainy days!) At times I used force to get people to clean their own living quarters or to help collect their own food....Sometimes I wondered why I stayed behind to help. Why, why, why was I made to regret it?...

He sounded very very tired and described how the refugees had just kept pouring in, month after month. Finally although weak, he and North left Shingbwiyang. The journey took them many days. Some of the time they appeared to follow an unknown route. It is not known if they had any maps but they must have had some supplies of food. As Katz said, he was near to death and he appears to have understated what he went through.

'...On September 17th after almost five months here, North and I left for Margherita...The Namyung river proved to be un-crossable, so we cut off to the left on to a jungle path which probably had not been used by a white man before. The journey was arduous. Mountains some 6000 ft to 7000 ft high had to be climbed. Makeshift bridges spanned many rivers. I felt scared and stumbled occasionally, but luck held and we made good progress. Climbing the largest mountain of 7000 ft almost brought about

my death. The climb down was the worst. My leg was twisted and I was in agony for two days. Altogether the journey took 20 days to travel over these mountains. It was hell while it lasted but we arrived in Margherita feeling comparatively better. I had actually put on some weight!..

...Mr 'Tommy' Thomson, the Refugee Adminstrator put us up. I've never met a kinder man! He was more than generous in his hospitality and nothing was too much trouble for him. He saw to all our needs at once and personally took us by car to the places we had to report to. I cannot sufficiently express my thanks! It was only now that we found out how big a part the people in India had played in the evacuation from Burma. Tommy Thomson told us the story of some of the problems that they had to deal with. I apologized for the nasty things I thought and said while in Shingbwiyang. We just did not know!

This Ted is the end of my story of the evacuation from Burma. It was not long before all the camps closed down. The remainder of the refugees at Shingbwiyang came through eventually. Reaction often set in. The refugees, after enduring untold horrors, arrived in India only to die of exhaustion. This to my mind was the biggest tragedy of the evacuation. I'm feeling dead inside and I'm now off to the hospital for a complete overhaul and later a holiday, I hope. Here is to forgetting all about the "Valley of Death"!

CHAPTER TWENTY SEVEN
May to November

Stories of Great Courage

From May the Indian Tea- planters' Association had turned the Margherita Golf Course and Polo Ground into a reception camp for refugees arriving from the Hukawng Valley, with many tents and an office in the old club house. Much thought and effort went into planning relief and rescue for refugees over this difficult, mountainous and rain sodden route, and it was a time when the organization was already overstretched from other similar operations.

There were other Tea-planters' camps already operating. When the refugee plane had landed in Dinjan, Assam with Dr Russell's wife on board, '... *a friendly English tea-planter in a homely green pork-pie hat stood ready to receive them...*' This was in late April. Josephine had written - '*May 22nd ....We arrived at 8 pm and had dinner in the Teaplanters' camp. So civilized and clean and comfortable.*'

At the end of May Dr Russell had become aware of the efforts of relief parties from Assam on their route. From Assam were brought fresh medical supplies, food and information about the track ahead. He wrote:: '*Henceforth, we were never to be out of reach of food or shelter. A proper rest-camp was situated about every ten miles, with lesser tea-camps at shorter intervals.*'

When they arrived at Margherita refugees were registered and divided into civilian or military groups. On June 11th Captain Gribble had just survived a terrifying experience on the rapids and he wrote '... *about 5 p.m. we landed near the railway bridge at Margherita and made our way to the Rest Camp in pouring rain...*'

In a remarkable book '*Forgotten Frontier*' (1945) Geoffrey Tyson wrote about the strain that was being put on the ITA when they first heard about the refugees coming through the Hukawng Valley in May. They felt they had to plan relief operations although as yet they only had approximate estimates of how many refugees there were on this route..

On May 6th an ITA liaison Officer and an officer of the Burma Service of Engineers set out to survey the route. They were fit and able to proceed along the mule track on both sides of the Pangsau Pass in a comparatively short time. The track had not yet deteriorated into the treacherous and slippery mountain path that it became later during the monsoon.

There were to be thousands more refugees than they expected. During a meeting on May 12th it was realized that this was a very difficult route indeed, and a huge effort was going to be required. As the operation got under way there was much attention to detail. Advance parties prepared to survey the route from Assam, with each party including ITA Liaison Officers, a surgeon or doctor and an assistant, twelve workers and fifty porters, usually Abors. Much equipment, medical aid and supplies had to be carried over the mountains. Members of the military were helping the relief effort but were often recalled by the army.

There had been mention of road building projects at both ends of the route but after some work had been done they were suspended or abandoned. In December 1941 Captain Gribble had been asked to supervise preparations for building a motor road through the dense forest country. He referred to '...*the countless numbers of coolies expected to arrive within twenty days for the purpose of constructing a main highway...* ' He had been surprised and overwhelmed with this task, as the local villagers were busy with cultivation at that time of the year. Not yet knowing about the thousands of refugees who would be converging on this track, he had asked – '.. *In what respect was this new road intended to assist the war effort?*' He knew that in a matter of weeks the jungle paths would be running with water.

However work did start: : '... *I was absent from Headquarters for nine days but in that short space of time over 500 members of the tribes with whom I was acquainted responded to the call, and were organized and distributed. Now they were working like ants, felling trees, building bridges, erecting bamboo sheds, and constructing rafts for use at river crossings where bridges were impossible.*

Although this work did not continue, it presumably made the first stages of the track more usable by motor transport and there were many stories of lorries and jeeps that were able to proceed for quite some miles in the first stage before having to be abandoned, as was the case in Dr Russell's group.

On April 30th Gribble was becoming aware of the huge numbers of refugees on the track and on May 4th he recorded that he inspected the work and paid Kachin villagers. As regards the workers intended to arrive from other locations, he finally wrote: '...*The Labour Corps was merely a dream, a fantasy, which vanished into thin air...* ' And by May 14th he had himself been drawn into the refugee journey and commented that there was no going back.

At the India end there were already some supply camps that had been created for workers on a road project. The ITA were planning to establish camps at intervals, but on the mountains and through dense, waterlogged jungle this was a very difficult task. On May 26th gangs of tea garden labour arrived from Doom-Dooma. Each day three hundred porters set out carrying supplies.

Labourers who were recruited to rescue and carry sick and exhausted refugees and to supply and maintain the camps on the track were often from the Tea plantations. Some were paid special rates for short periods, and were working under planters they knew personally. Dr Russell wrote: '...*A long string of stocky little Abor coolies came into the camp carrying heavy bags of rice. They wore little beyond a loin-cloth, a dah and an intriguing hat made of cane shaped very like a bowler, and so stoutly woven that it was proof against a lusty sword-cut – the Naga equivalent of the 'Battle bowler' of civilization...*'

There were also Garos, Pnars and Khasis who often worked under officers they did not know personally. Some porters deserted when in Naga country as they had heard stories of *'head choppings'* and the difficulties of the track affected all the relief parties, many of whom also suffered from illness, with some losing their lives.

But for the refugees on the track the sight of the porters approaching with supplies and information from Assam gave them huge encouragement. And there were stories of relief workers going out with lanterns long after nightfall to bring people to the camps who had fallen exhausted by the wayside.

Communication along the tortuous route was very difficult and many extra journeys had to be made on foot between the camps. By the last week in May there was wireless communication between Nampong and Ledo, although with limited equipment. This was brought by Captain A Ramsay Tainsh, a young regular Army officer attached to the Supply Department. He was energetic and decisive and reduced looting and volunteered for many tasks and later wrote a book - *'And Some Fell by the Wayside - An Account of the North Burma Evacuation 1942'.*

By June 1st there was a system of camps established and during the first week 10,000 evacuees travelled through, with the highest figure being 7,355 in one day at Nampong. There was a story of a doctor from the Nampong camp carrying a seriously ill refugee on his back who the porters had refused to help. However morale was usually high within the relief workers, and the Road Commander at Nampong founded the *'Jeep Club'* with its own insignia of strands of cane worn below the knee in the

Naga style.

However, through June and July the ITA operation reached a crisis point. Heavy rain was almost continuous. Based on what few facts were known at the time, it was decided to close some camps towards the end of June. The track was ruined and finding porters was almost impossible. The sickness rate amongst the porters was around 50% and in one week alone 23 deaths were reported.

After much brave work the Abors were released from duty as porters. There were risks of camp staff themselves being completely cut off and falling ill. It was wrongly assumed that there were to be no more refugees coming through. The conditions made the storing of food difficult, though in fact there were still some stocks of food at Nampong and the R.A.F were still dropping food at Shingbwiyang and Tagap Ga.

But much to the anxiety of the planners, the stream of refugees did not cease, but came and went, influenced partly by changes in the weather. There was a break in the rain from June $17^{th} - 20^{th}$. As Katz so vividly described, the situation was complicated by the arrival at various camps of large numbers of hungry Chinese troops. Some camps were withdrawn and some re-organised.

It was around this time (June 9th) that Katz received the contradictory message at Shwingbwiyang telling all refugees not to proceed further, and at the same time advising that any officers at the camp were to consider that they had no further duties to perform, and advising them to make their own way to India by whichever route they could and seek the assistance of the Chinese Fifth Army.

For thousands of refugees it was a terrible drawn out journey with an uncertain outcome. The ITA relief work needed to keep going, finding more workers with difficulty. On June 26th it was agreed to bring in 200 Assam Rifles from Sadiya, and they were to make one trip over the track doing what they could. They were fit and adaptable, though hampered by having no porters to assist them.

There were many dilemmas. It was difficult to decide whether to treat refugees en route. Inoculations against cholera could be done, with some 'patching up' of the terrible sores that developed, but significant medical facilities could not be carried all the way to many of the camps.

There were heartrending decisions to be made about who could survive being carried for many miles on stretchers and who was just too ill to justify the considerable effort of attempting this. Worn out refugees were encouraged and often almost forced to move on, as to pause in the disease ridden damp conditions often led to a worsening in their mental and physical condition.

As time went on those arriving in Assam were in a worse state than ever, with starvation and illness associated with vitamin deficiency added to the already long list of problems. Many tragically died after reaching the final ITA camp. Many had been walking for weeks and months, some from distant parts of Burma in the heat before the monsoon.

The relief workers kept going through the months, saving many lives. There were stories of great courage. Then some workers were needed to build airfields in Assam. The ITA was running out of manpower. There is a complicated account in a report written by K. J. Lindop who was himself involved in relief expeditions. This reveals the heroism of many relief parties, and happened later in November long after many camps had been closed down.

Rumours had reached the rescue parties that Shingbwiyang was being cleared of refugees. A group went to Nawngyang. '...*On the 5th of November on a sweep forward to Tagung Hka the lately in Charge Officer – Captain B, Tagap Ga – was met on the road and our worst fears were realized when it was learnt that he had left Tagap Ga...an unknown number of refugees estimated by him at 200, without rations.   ...Mr N.A.B.Warner at once volunteered to lead a relief party in a dash to Tagap Ga with rations.*

A party of porters were chosen, the minimum requirements of the relief party were carefully worked out;   loads were weighed and packed and by 13.30 hrs on the 6th November, the party accompanied by two Sepoys of the Assam Rifles was ready to take to the road.

Tagung Hka was reached at dusk, the track having been made damnable by rain and a large number of refugees were found there. From the fastest amongst them, it was learnt that there were some 200 persons on the road on the India side of Tagap Ga.

A second party of 10 porters under the writer accompanied the relief party as far as Ngalang Ga, carrying one day's rations for the relief party and the 110 refugees they were expected to bring out.

On the 7th November, after clearing Tagung Hka of refugees, both parties marches to Ngalang Ga, where the day's rations for the returning expedition were carefully hidden in the jungle.   Mr Warner and his relief army then went on to camp at Namlip and to reach Tagap Ga on the 8th.   The writer and his party returned to Tagung Hka.

At Ngalang Ga starving refugees were found in the last stages of exhaustion with a dead girl in their midst.   Before the returning party was ready to leave a Sepoy died, leaving the 10 porters and one Sepoy of the Assam Rifles faced with the task of moving 7 practically helpless people over 8 miles of track made like ice by rain.

That they did it – six of the porters, not only making Tagung Hka with their stretcher cases, but coming back 3 miles of stiff climb in the dark to help in the rest of the party – is an example of the magnificent work done throughout by the Tea Garden Labour.'

Another incident gives a glimpse of the endurance and stamina of the relief parties. *'...rations for a probably 300-400 refugees, as well as for the Tea Garden coolies, had to be rushed up over the long steep climb over the Pangsau Pass from Nampong. At the same time, both Nawngyang and Nampong camps had to be evacuated to make room for the expected influx of refugees. Captain Sawyer and A. Munro at Nampong, T.E Carroll at Nawngyang and the porters at both camps responded to this heavy call. For several days officers and porters travelled backwards and forwards over the Pass, loaded in both directions, until Nawngyang was restocked with rations and clear of refugees. During this period Tagung Hka was also restocked.'*

There were many more details in Lindop's report: *'With the arrival of the relief party at Nawngyang the road from Shingbwiyang had been cleared, with the exception of some 30 refugees too ill to survive the journey, seen between Shingbwiyang and Tagap Ga. These were some 26 Punjabis and Madrassi at Tagap Ga, who refused to move, and 4 Gurkhas passed on the road who were travelling at their own speed.*

Preparations were at once put in hand for the withdrawal of the road organization, stage by stage, to the base....On the 19th November a final sweep forward as far as the water on the Ngalang Ga hill was made, resulting in the bringing in of 7 refugees, including the above mentioned Gurkhas.

On the 20th November the Burma Flag was struck at Nawngyang and everyone moved back over the frontier to Nampong. Each camp was dealt with in turn as had been done at Nawngyang. Nampong was evacuated on the 24th, Namchik on the 26th, Kumlao on the 28th and the whole party reached the rail-head at Tipong, and eventually Margherita the same night... During the team's tour of duty on the road, deaths were remarkably few. At Ngalang Ga there were 4; at Tagung Hka – 2; at Nawngyang – 4; at Namlip – 1; at Nampong – 4; at Namchik – 1 at Kumlao – 1' a total of 17.

To these must be added Cpl. Meaton R.A.M.C. who disappeared between Tagap Ga and Ngalang Ga. These figures suggest very forcibly that the fearful casualty lists of July and August might have been avoided had the road been kept patrolled and supplied with food throughout the monsoon rains.

Lindop ended his report with the words:...*In conclusion. I would say that for those who saw them, the hundreds of graveless dead, lining and in places paving the track, will long remain a ghastly memory. To each one of us came the question of whether more might not have been done to help, if the actual conditions of the track had been realized earlier and the rescue team had come sooner on the scene.'*

CHAPTER TWENTY EIGHT
December 1942 – June 1944

The Ledo Road

'...*The whole of the Hukawng Valley has been a battleground, a battle against the Japanese, mosquitoes and leeches. We can well imagine men fighting and marching blindly through hundreds of miles of rough, rocky, forest-clad country where the sky seldom shows...*'
Captain Gribble (1944)

In these parts of Burma various road building projects had been started and abandoned during the previous year. However in December 1942, a year after these stories began and a month after the closing down of the drawn out and exhausting relief work of the ITA, work began on building the Ledo Road. It was to follow the very track which had been used by thousands of refugees.

The Burma Road supply route to China had been blocked when the Japanese captured Rangoon in March, and there was an urgent need for a supply road to China. The U S were continually helping the Chinese war effort against the Japanese and supplies from the U S were being been flown 'over the Hump' to China. This was a massive operation involving dangerous flights from India over the high mountains of the eastern Himalayas in unpredictable weather and without navigation aids.

The new road from Ledo in Assam would have to climb over the Pangsau Pass and the mountains and down to the Hukawng valley and pass through Shingbwiyang and Myitkyina. Although British railway builders had surveyed the high Pangsau Pass in the 19th century, no railway had been built at this time. Also road builders had considered that a road down into the Hukawng Valley was a possibility. Now during the war this road became a priority.

15000 American soldiers and tens of thousands of local workers set to work at a cost $150 million. Many died during its construction with ever present dangers of war and the extreme difficulties of the terrain. Because of the the inaccessible jungle and mountains information about local conditions could only be acquired as the road building progressed.

It was a huge undertaking and the road, along with the Burma Road to which it was later joined, was eventually renamed the Stilwell Road. In December 1942 the Supreme Commander in the Far East British General Sir Archibald Wavell agreed with General Stilwell to make the Ledo Road an American NCAC operation.

Work started on the first section, following the steep narrow refugee trail across the Patkai Range and through the Pangsau Pass ('Hell Pass') and down to Shingbwiyang. 100,000 cubic feet of earth per mile had to be shifted. Massive amounts of equipment had to be brought in, shipped over from the U S.

In this part of the road there were steep gradients, hairpin bends and sheer drops of hundreds of feet, surrounded by dense rain forest. Mules slipped in the mud and Japanese snipers hid in the trees behind Allied lines frequently killing workers on the road. There was the constant battle with illness, extremes of climate and the horrific conditions in the jungle.

The road reached Shingbwiyang on Dec 27th 1943. From Shingbwiyang there was a track which the Japanese had improved which was used. Two fuel pipe lines were laid along this section of the road.

465 miles from Ledo at the Mong-Yu junction the new road met the old Burma Road. It was a major achievement. It had crossed 10 major rivers and 155 smaller streams. Supplies could gradually be brought along the road to areas such as Kamaing, Mogaung and Myitkyina. Supplies were still being flown over the Hump, though by this time with the use of more modern transport aircraft.

Some sections of the Ledo road in the Hukawng Valley soon needed repair because of heavy monsoon rains. But eventually the 1079 miles of road linked India to China, and the first convoy of vehicles left Ledo in 1945 on Jan.12th, reaching Kunming in China on Feb 4th. In the next 6 months trucks carried 129,000 tons of supplies from India to China, and thousands of trucks that had carried the cargo were then handed over to the Chinese.

There was a sign at the beginning of the Ledo Road which read:
Ledo Assam 0 Shingbwiyang 103 Warazup 189 Myitkyina 268 Bhamo 372 Wanting 507 Lunfling 560 Paoshan 652 Yungping 755 Yunnanyi 876 Tsuyung 959 Kunming 1079

The Ledo Road had a significant impact on the progress of the war in this part of Burma, but despite the huge effort and expense of building it and the many lives lost, it is now unused and overgrown.

In June 1944 Captain Gribble wrote: *"The monsoon in North Burma has now started in earnest rendering operations more difficult. Chinese and American troops fighting their way forward have advanced two miles south of the Kamaing-Mogaung Road in north Burma. One hundred enemy soldiers were killed near Kamaing."*

This bald report in a newspaper dated June 1944 does not of course convey any hint or suggestion regarding the magnitude of the fighting in that jungle country. The whole of the Hukawng Valley has been a battleground, a battle against the Japanese, mosquitoes and leeches. We can well imagine men fighting and marching blindly through hundreds of miles of rough, rocky, forest-clad country where the sky seldom shows.

The story when written will disclose amazing feats of endurance; with the impossible having been made possible during those ghastly months. And through it all our Kachins and Nagas fought alongside Chinese, American and British forces, helping them to destroy the Japanese invaders.

We are happier now that we know the stream of life begins to swing back into Burma along a new 'Ledo Road'. Life will soon flow again back to (and beyond) the little fishing village of Kamaing where those kindly, loveable people will once more gather in the little churches to the slow deep booming of a Burmese gong.

EPILOGUE in 2014

In Kachin State is Myanmar's highest mountain, Hkakabo Razi (19,000 ft) at the southern tip of the Himalayas. It is a resource rich region sharing important borders with China and India. The Kachin people are known for their disciplined fighting skills, inter-clan relations, herbal healing, craftsmanship and jungle survival skills. There are a number of ethnic sub groups, some of whom also live in China and India.

After the third Anglo-Burmese war when all of Burma was ruled by the British (1886-1948) most of the Kachin territory was administered as a frontier region. Kachin troops formed a significant part of the Burmese Army. Christianity spread and is still practiced today, but is part of the reasons why Kachins are now discriminated against by the Burmese government.

The Kachins were one of the ethnic minorities who signed the Panglong Agreement of 1947 before General Aung San was assassinated. They received approval for the creation of a separate Kachin State, and after independence they were not immediately involved in ethnic insurgencies.

In 1961 Buddhism was declared as the official religion of Burma. At the time of General Ne Win's military coup in 1962 the President-elect was a

Kachin, Sama Duwa Sinwa Nawng. Kachins were discriminated against and this led to the forming of the Kachin Independence Organization (KIO), and its armed wing, the KIA, which grew into one of the largest ethnic resistance forces in the country.

In 1994 the KIO signed a ceasefire agreement with the military regime and was granted some of its own administrative rights. However the fundamental grievances of the KIA were not addressed, and discrimination continued, with many ethnic Burmese being appointed to administrative positions. There have been huge scale displacements of the population due to land confiscations, gold mining in the Hukawng valley and building projects, with forced labour and pressure for Christians to convert to Buddhism.

The Constitution of 2008 does not protect the rights of ethnic minorities in Myanmar, and proposals put forward by the minorities were rejected by the government.

In 2009 the regime issued a demand that ethnic groups including the KIA transform themselves into Border Guard Forces under the control of the Burmese Army. In 2011 the Burma Army launched an attack on the KIA, breaking the ceasefire agreement and the area remains unstable. Thousands of Kachins have been displaced.

MISCELLANEOUS PHOTOS OF BURMA

Old photo of the terraces at the Shwedagon Pagoda, Rangoon (dml)

Pagodas   (sfr)

A market in Maymyo (dml)

Schoolchildren in colonial days   (dml)

A ruby mine at Mogok   (dml)

A street in Mandalay (dml)

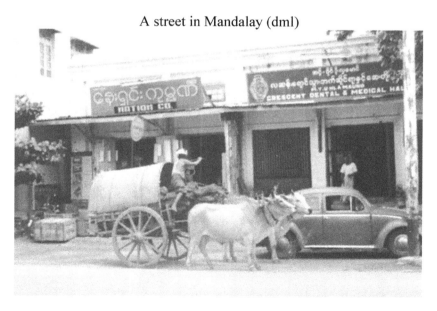

187

A hospital in Burma   (sfr)

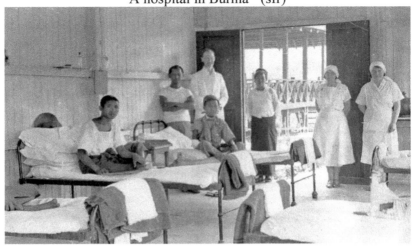

Dr Russell treating a patient   (pr)

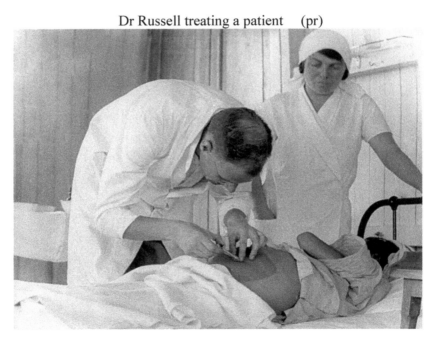

Hospital staff   (sfr)

Paddy fields   (dml)

Old train   (sfr)

Burmese landscape   (sfr)

Ted Rushton, Wilfred Crittle and George Tidey at the ITA
camp at S. Tirap, June 2nd 1942   (sfr)

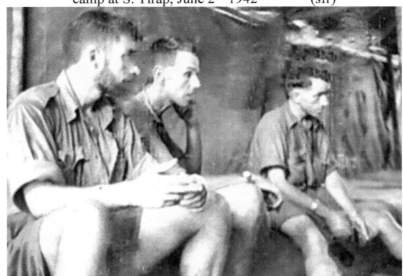

Caring for the pack animals

Dr Russell's group   (sfr)

A Jinghpaw (Kachin) guide with Gribble's party (sfr)

195

Burmese script   (etg)

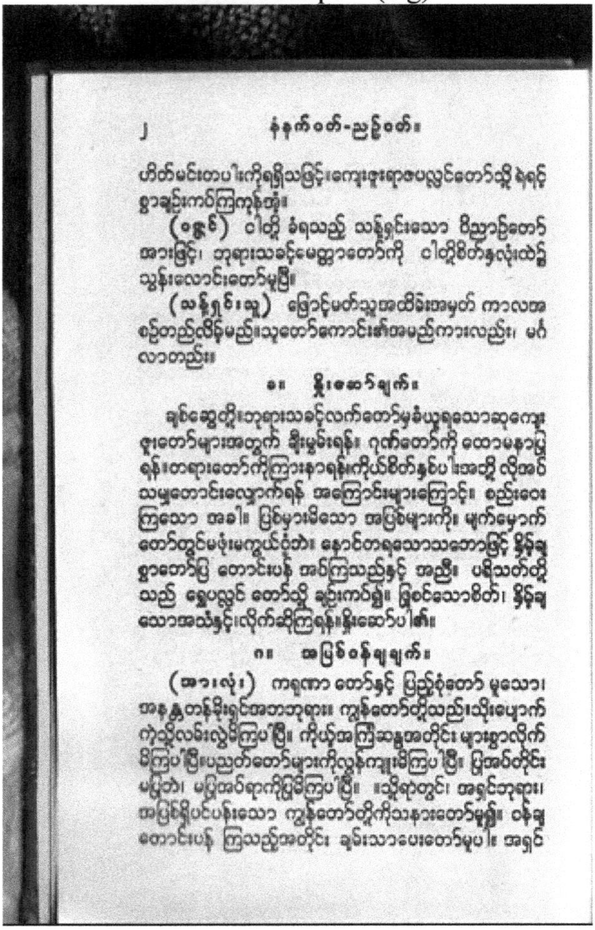

ဟိတ်မင်းတပါးကိုရှရှိသဖြင့်၊ကျေးဇူးရှာ၀လွင်တော်သို့ ရဲရင့်
စွာချဉ်းကင်ကြကုန်အံ့။

(ဝဋ္ဌာန်) ငါ့တို့ ခံရသည့် သန္တွင်းသော ပိညာဉ်တော်
အားဖြင့်၊ ဘုရားသခင်မေတ္တာတော်ကို ငါတို့စိတ်နှလုံးထဲ၌
သွန်းလောင်းတော်မူပြီ။

(သန္ရှင်းသူ) ဖြေ၁င့်မတ်သူ့အထိခိုးအမှတ် ကာလအ
စဉ်တည်လိမ့်မည်။သူတော်ကောင်းစ်၏အမည်ကားလည်း၊ မင်္ဂ
လာတည်း။။

၃။   မိုးဆောင်ချက်။

ချင်ဆွေတို့၊ဘုရားသခင့်လက်တော်မှခံယူရသောဆုကျေး
ဇူးတော်များအတွက် ဒိုးမွမ်းရန်၊ ဂုဏ်တော်ကို ထော၁နာပွ
ရန်၊တရားတော်ကိုကြ၁းနာရန်၊ကိုယ်စိတ်နှင်ပါ၊အ၁တို့ လိုအဝ်
သမ္မဒောင်လျှောက်ရန် အကြောင်းများကြောင့်။ စည်းဝေး
ကြသော အခါ၊ ပြစ်မှာမိသော အပြစ်များကို၊ မျက်မှောက်
တော်တွင်ဝန်ုံ့မကွယ်ငံ့တံ။ နောင်တ၁ရသောသဘော၁ဖြင့် ရှိုရ်ချ
စွ၁တော်ပြု တောင်းပန် အပ်ကြသည်နှင့် အညီ။ ပရိသတ်တို့
သည် ရွှေပလွင် တော်သို့ ခည်းကပ်၍၊ ခြွင်းသောမိတ်၊ ရှိုရ်ချ
သော၁အသံနှင့်၊လိုက်ဆိုကြရန်၊မိုးဆော၁ပ၁၏။။

၄။   အပြစ်ဝန်ချချက်။

(အ၁းလုံး) ကရုဏ၁ တော်နှင့် ပြည့်စုံတော် မူသော၊
အနန္တတန်ခိုးရှင်အ၁ဘုရား၊ ကျွန်တော်တို့သည်၊သိုးပျောက်
ကဲ့သို့လမ်းလွဲကြပ၁ပြီ၊ ကိုယ့်အကြံဆန္ဒအတိုင်း၊ မ၁းစွ၁လိုက်
မိကြပ၁ပြီ၊ပညတ်တော်များကိုလွန်ကျုးမိကြပ၁ပြီ၊ ပြုအပ်တိုင်း
မပြုဘဲ၊ မပြုအပ်ရာကိုပြုမိကြပ၁ပြီ။ သို့ရ၁တွင်၊ အရှင်ဘုရား၊
အပြစ်ဒိုပင်ပါးသော ကျွန်တော်တို့ကိုသနားတော်မူ၍၊ ဝန်ချ
တောင်းပန် ကြသည်အတိုင်း၊ ခွင်းသ၁ပေးတော်မူပ၁။ အရှင်

Old poster displayed in April 1   (sfr)

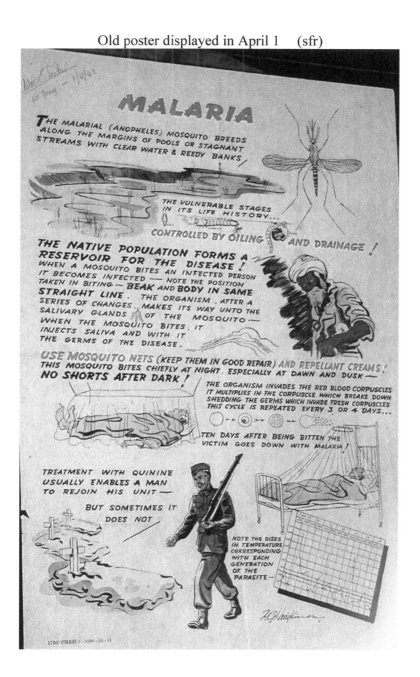

Index of some of the many individuals who appear in various accounts of the Evacuation of Burma

Appleton, Rev George went to Burma 1927, rural missionary Irrawaddy Delta. Appointed Warden of St John's College, Rangoon five years later. Flew out of Myitkyina 1942, was Director of Public Relations for Burma Government in Exile, Archdeacon of Rangoon 1943-46. Became Archbishop of Perth, Australia 1963 and Archbishop of Jerusalem in 1969. Appears Josephine's diary.

Bald, Lillian teacher (possibly the head teacher) Bishop's Home school, mentioned Josephine's story when they were still in Burma and trying to get children to safety, got separated from Josephine, later died in Hukawng Valley having written agonized letter asking for help. Appears *'Exodus Burma – The British Escape through the Jungles of Death 1942'*

Cam, Miss Avice, SPG missionary and nursing sister, worked in the Irrawaddy Delta and Mandalay, appears Josephine's diary and *'Weathering the storm'* (1946)

Chapman, Miss Josephine mother of author, Elizabeth Tebby Germaine. Worked in Burma for SPG society, wrote detailed diary from Dec.1941, witnessed bombing of Rangoon and Mandalay, walked out of Burma reaching Imphal May 21st, taught in India during the war and returned to Burma Dec. 1945, wrote a book *'Weathering the Storm – the story of the Church in Burma'* (1946). Fluent Burmese speaker, recorded war experiences of Burmese and Karens and wrote post war descriptions of Burma. 1947 married Christopher Lewis who is mentioned in her diary Feb 26th . 1949 the family with young baby escaped from civil war Maymyo, returned to England 1951

Chapman, Lt. Colonel Melrose, b.1887 An older half- brother of Josephine, Indian army, in 1942 responsible for supplies and transport in Burma, sent her coded message February saying route through Toungoo was unsafe. Distinguished military career, awarded D.S.O. 1917 in the Somme, French War Cross 1918. Served France and Flanders 1915 and 1917/18, Germany 1918/1919 and India from 1928, Burma from 1937

Crittle, Rev Wilfred worked for over 15 years with Kachin Christians in remote village of Kamaing, neighbour of Captain Gribble, travelled through jungle at different times with both with Dr Russell and Captain Gribble. Wrote account *'The Evacuation from Northern Burma and the trek to India',* In March/April 1942 wrote *'I had not been long back from Mohnyin when I had a visit from Brooks of the SPG who was sent up by the Bishop's commissary to make enquiries concerning the possibility of our being able to accommodate some of the SPG lady workers should they have to evacuate from central Burma. We gave him details of the accommodation at our disposal and expressed our willingness to receive the ladies should occasion arise.'* (This might have included Josephine had circumstances been different)

'Exodus Burma – The British Escape through the Jungles of Death 1942' (2011) book by Felicity Goodall. Very detailed book contains many extracts from diaries and letters. Miss Chapman is described in diary of Fred Tizzard, a captain of the Irrawaddy Flotilla Company. *'...Then there is Miss Chapman in short blue skirt and blouse, shoes that seem suitable, but may not have 200 miles wear left in them. She is a Missionary, one in charge of a Rangoon orphan's home. Her orphans went up to Myitkyina to fly out. She is short, fit and hardy. No nonsense about her, full of confidence.'* In diary Josephine mentioned an IFC captain on May 19th (which may be the same person). Later Josephine appears to have been an active member of the walking group – Tizzard wrote: *'...We had to be content with a place where fire had swept through a bamboo thicket, leaving the ground thick with ashes and the bamboos blackened. From the stream I lever up stones to Miss Chapman...'* Also mentioned briefly in this book are: Dr Russell and his group, George Tidey, Lillian Bald, Benjamin Katz, Major Alastair Tainsh, Rev and Mrs Darlington, Neil North, Father Stuart and many others

Garrad, Padre William worked for many years in Burma. Appears Josephine's diary, she accompanied him on visit to Sagaing during bombing of Mandalay in April, flew out of Myitkyina.

Gribble, Captain R H ('Reggie') worked for Burma Frontier service based in remote village of Kamaing, neighbour of Rev Wilfred Crittle, travelled with mule train through Hukawng valley, knew many Kachin and Naga chiefs and villagers, was helped by them on his journey, wrote book *'Out of the Burma Night'* (1944) published by Thacker Spink & Co, Calcutta

Katz, Sergeant Benjamin, RAMC Orderly who stayed to help refugees at Shingbwiyang May – September 1942. He and Neil North supported each other through difficulties and illnesses. Became Refugee Officer, then was appointed Camp Commandant of Shingbwiyang by Neil North. Anglo-Polish Jew from Liverpool, later worked for colonial services and married an Anglo-Indian. Wrote a remarkable *'Letter from Shingbwiyang'* to 'Ted' describing the horrors of the situation.

Lewis, Rev Christopher SPG missionary, father of author Elizabeth Tebby Germaine, mentioned Josephine's diary Feb 26th on his own trek out of Burma with his sister Dorothy.

Lewis, Miss Dorothy (dml) worked for SPG in Burma in 30's and after war until 1966, friend and future sister in law of Josephine Chapman, appears diary Feb.26th on her journey out of Burma with her brother, Christopher, took many photos of Burma

North, Neil (Cornelius) Deputy Commissioner for Myitkyina district. Recruited to Colonial Service 1939, posted Burma 1940, and to Myitkyina 1941. Stayed behind in Shinbwiyang in 1942 to supervise thousands of refugees flooding through the village and was later awarded the M.B.E. in Jan 1943. After monsoon ended, walked to India with Benjamin Katz, arriving Oct 4th. Returned to Burma 1943 as Kachin Liaison Officer with the Chindits, spoke the language. Appointed Aide de Camp to General Wingate early 1944. Later wounded and taken to hospital at Shillong, India where he was cared for by Dr Russell. I944 returned to Shingbwiyang along newly built Ledo road, later became Civil Officer, and later posted to Lauhkang on the North East Frontier of India. Later worked Tanzania, Sudan and Kenya, ICI England. Obtained doctorate 1996, died April 11, 2011. Dr Russell's son Rev Paul Russell visited Neil and his wife and was lent suitcase of historic records of the Evacuation of Burma by the widow of Neil's neighbour, 'Tommy' Thompson (R M Thompson of the Indian Tea-planters' Association)

Russell F.R.C.S., Stanley Farrant worked as surgeon Mohnyin hospital from 1930, walked out of Burma, 1942, worked at Shillong hospital until 1947 when family returned to England. Appears in several accounts of the evacuation of Burma. Wrote *'Muddy Exodus A story of the Evacuation of Burma, May 1942'* (1943) published by The Epworth Press, London, and *'Over the Hills and Far Away'* (an account of the experiences of his wife and family)

Sein, Ma Pwa mentioned Josephine's diary, Feb 5th.   A highly respected and loved Burmese head teacher at St Mary's SPG school, Kemmendine, Rangoon. In Feb 1942 aged about 48 she advised Josephine not to tour any more. From a strong Buddhist family who initially disowned her when she converted to Christianity. In *'Weathering the Storm'* Josephine wrote about her life, and her tragic death during the war at the hands of Burmese Buddhists who heard that she had helped British soldiers.

Simmonds, Miss Rosina, SPG nurse, appears Josephine's diary

Tainsh, Major A.R.   was responsible for aiding refugees who came over the Pangsau Pass – wrote a book *'And Some Fell by the Wayside   - An Account of the North Burma Evacuation'* (1948) published by Orient Longmans

Tidey, Rev George Archdeacon of Rangoon, walked out of Burma mainly with Dr Russell's group, wrote extensive diary, appears in Josephine's diary

Thomson I.T.A., Mr R M, 'Tommy' Thomson, Administrator of the Refugee Camp at the Margherita Golf Course and Polo Ground, organized the difficult operation to rescue refugees from the Hukawng Valley. Had suitcase of papers which were lent to Paul Russell and have been used in the writing of this book.

Websper, Evelyn SPG nurse/midwife, worked in Irrawaddy Delta, flew out from Myitkyina, appears Josephine's diary and George Tidey's diary

Also by this author:

HOW TO PLAY THE PIANO   BOOK 1
Grade 5–8 – unique scale charts, arpeggio exercises and chord routines
which will make piano music easier to learn and understand

HOW TO PLAY THE PIANO   BOOK 2
Grade 5–8 – ways to develop skills and effective practising

HOW TO PLAY THE PIANO   BOOK 3
Grade 5 - 8 -   a guide to the classical repertoire – lists of over 600 graded
pieces by many composers

REALLY USEFUL VIOLIN DUETS
 – beginners to grade 3
ISBN   978 1 78610 176 1

REALLY USEFUL VIOLA DUETS
- beginners to grade 3
ISBN   978 1 78610 227 0

 'DISTANT AND DANGEROUS DAYS IN BURMA AND CHINA'
third edition published 2014